映画で学ぶ 英語を楽しむ

English Delight of Movie English and TOEIC

高瀬文広
[編]

Kate Parkinson
[英文校閲]

ミネルヴァ書房

まえがき

　英語を楽しく，そして楽に学習できるテキストはないものかと考えて作成したのが，*English Delight of Movie English and TOEIC* です。本書は映画を英語教育，異文化理解，そして対人コミュニケーション等に如何にして利用するかを研究している映画英語教育学会の九州支部ならびにアメリカ映画文化学会の会員により執筆されたものです。

　本書は映画を利用して，TOEIC の試験対策もできる画期的なテキストとなっています。本書で取り扱っている映画は 2013 年前後に上映された非常に新しいものばかりで，授業で使用する DVD も容易に手に入れることができます。本書のもう一つの特色として，各 Unit の末に Trivia & Goofs というコラムを入れていることです。Trivia として映画の雑学的知識となるあまり知られていない事実や秘話を掲載し，映画の面白さを知ってもらえるようにしました。

　また Goofs，これは映画を制作する過程で生じた映画の中の間違いシーンです。本当は有るはずなのに映像の次の場面では消えていたりする事物，その映画が取り上げている時代にはまだ発明されていなかったものや，事実と異なっているものを紹介しているコーナーです。

　このような Trivia & Goofs を使って，映画の中の間違いシーンをクイズ形式で探させたり答えさせたりする学習者の意欲を高めるような授業に利用すると，アクティブ・ラーニングの一環として授業にアクセントをつけ，さらに楽しいものにすることができます。

　本書では全部で 16 本の映画を取り上げ，16 の Unit で下記のような構成にしています。

【本文構成】

Vocabulary：各 Unit の映画に関する英語での説明文中に出てくる読解に必要な重要語句を事前に確認できるようになっています。

Reading：全部で 16 本の映画を Unit に分け，各 Unit にそれぞれ映画の中に存在するモチーフや内容をテーマとして取り上げて説明するとともに，その映画の制作に関することや映画のあらすじ，そして，映画の見所等をわかりやすい英文で説明しています。

Comprehension Check：本文の内容をどれ位理解できているかを top-down 形式で 4 問～ 5 問程度の内容把握問題にしています。

For TOEIC：TOEIC の試験を意識して 3 つの設問から構成されています。設問 3 は TOEIC の Part 5 形式の問題，設問 4 は TOEIC の Part 7 形式の問題，そして設問 5 は TOEIC の Part 6 形式の問題となっています。映画の内容に合わせた問題となっており，楽しみながら TOEIC 対策ができます。

Trivia & Goofs
　Trivia：映画の雑学的知識となるあまり知られていない事実や秘話。
　Goofs：映画を制作する過程で生じた映画の中の間違いシーン。

　最後に，本書刊行にあたりミネルヴァ書房編集部の浅井久仁人さんには大変お世話になりました。
　この場を借りて深甚の謝意を表します。

編者　　高瀬　文広
アメリカ映画文化学会 会長
映画英語教育学会 九州支部長

CONTENTS

Unit 1 Country Music / *Country Strong* ·· 1

Unit 2 The Grimm Fairy Tales / *Tangled* ··· 7

Unit 3 Religious Faith / *Life of Pi* ·· 13

Unit 4 Automaton / *Hugo* ·· 19

Unit 5 Environmental Problem / *No Impact Man* ································ 25

Unit 6 Asian Disciple to Reach Maturity / *The Karate Kid* ····················· 31

Unit 7 Bioengineering and Society / *The Amazing Spider-Man* ·············· 37

Unit 8 Complex and Pride / *The King's Speech* ··································· 43

Unit 9 Major League Baseball / *Moneyball* ··· 49

Unit 10 Business / *The Social Network* ·· 55

Unit 11 Psychological Test Subjects / *The Experiment* ·························· 61

Unit 12 Aroma / *Spy Kids 4D : All the Time in the World* ······················ 67

Unit 13 Dangerous Food Supply / *Food, Inc.* ······································ 73

Unit 14 Wolf & Witch-hunting / *Red Riding Hood* ······························· 79

Unit 15 Self-searching Journey / *Eat, Pray, Love* ································· 85

Unit 16 Travelling in Space / *Gravity* ·· 91

執筆者紹介
（執筆順）

高瀬文広（たかせ・ふみひろ，福岡医療短期大学） 編者
吉村　圭（よしむら・けい，鹿児島女子短期大学） Unit 1
Nikandrov Nikolai（ニカンドロフ・ニコライ，福岡医療短期大学） Unit 2
鶴田里美香（つるた・りみか，シネマアナリスト） Unit 3
鶴田知嘉香（つるた・ちかこ，福岡常葉高等学校） Unit 4
八尋春海（やひろ・はるみ，西南女学院大学） Unit 5
大木正明（おおき・まさあき，大分工業高等専門学校） Unit 6
藤山和久（ふじやま・かずひさ，熊本高等専門学校） Unit 7
中村茂徳（なかむら・しげのり，西南女学院大学） Unit 8
山崎祐一（やまさき・ゆういち，長崎県立大学） Unit 9
岡崎修平（おかざき・しゅうへい，英語講師） Unit 10
山下友子（やました・ゆうこ，九州大学） Unit 11
イネス多恵子（いねす・たえこ，Guilford College of Aromatherapy） Unit 12
鹿子木一郎（かなこぎ・いちろう，福岡県立筑紫高等学校） Unit 13
Linda 文子 鹿子木（りんだ・あやこ・かなこぎ，福岡医療短期大学） Unit 13
村田希巳子（むらた・きみこ，北九州市立大学） Unit 14
篠原一英（しのはら・かずひで，福岡県立久留米高等学校） Unit 15
浦田毅彦（うらた・たけひこ，福岡市立壱岐中学校） Unit 16

英文校閲
Kate Parkinson（ケイト・パーキンソン，福岡大学）

イラスト
きたむらイラストレーション　北村信明

Unit 1
Country Music

Vocabulary

1．本文中に登場する次の (1) 〜 (7) の語彙と同じような意味になるものを，下の (a) 〜 (g) から選びなさい。

（1） reputation （a） 移　民
（2） rural （b） 特　徴
（3） immigrant （c） 田舎の
（4） distinctive （d） 忘れられない
（5） feature （e） 貧　困
（6） memorable （f） 名　声
（7） poverty （g） 特色のある

Reading

Country Strong portrays the agony of a country music singer. Kelly Canter is a country music superstar who has won Grammy awards six times and Platinum Records seven times. However, in the opening scene of this film, she is forced to live in a rehabilitation facility. About a year ago her alcoholism caused a nervous breakdown.
5 Kelly got drunk and fell off the stage during a concert. Her husband is called James, and he is also her manager. James decides to organize a nationwide concert tour for Kelly. She leaves the rehabilitation facility for the tour, even though she has not fully recovered. Her reputation and recovery depend on whether the tour will be successful or not.

Country music originated in the southern United States during the 1920s. "Country"
10 means "rural", and as the name indicates, country music has its roots in the folk music of rural Georgia. During this time, the mostly white, working class Americans blended popular songs, Irish and Celtic fiddle tunes, traditional ballads, and cowboy songs. Also, immigrants from Europe added their own musical traditions into the mix. Now, the term "country music" is used to describe many styles and varieties of music.

15 Although there are many varieties of country music today, they share some common features. Most country music sounds very distinctive because of its combination of banjos, guitars, and fiddles; instruments introduced by working class laborers from rural Georgia, Africa, and Europe. A lot of country music is played to an energetic "square dance" rhythm; from a time when such music was the only form of
20 entertainment for many rural communities.

During the rest of the twentieth century, country music spread across the United States, and then around the world. Country Music arrived in Japan in 1971, when John Denver's *Take Me Home, Country Roads* became a worldwide hit. The song was covered by Olivia Newton-John two years later, and this cover version became a hit in Japan in
25 1995, when it featured in the Studio Ghibli animation *Whisper of the Heart*. In that movie, the heroine, Shizuku, translates the lyrics of the song into Japanese and sings the translated version in a memorable scene. Despite its age, this song remains one of the best known, and best loved country songs in Japan.

Country Strong portrays another feature often found in country music: the blues.
30 Working class life in rural Georgia was filled with hardship and poverty, so it is not surprising that a lot of country music focuses on these themes. Kelly Canter's struggles with her fading career, her alcoholism, and her failing marriage represent a modern day version of the difficulties experienced by the original country music musicians a century ago.

Comprehension Check

2．本文の内容と一致するものには〇，一致しないものには×をつけなさい。
(1)【　】ケリーは十分に快復しないまま施設を出ることになった。
(2)【　】カントリーミュージックは主にヨーロッパからの移民が様々な音楽を混ぜて作りあげた音楽ジャンルだ。
(3)【　】現在，カントリーミュージックには非常に多くの種類があるので，それぞれの楽曲に共通する特徴を見つけるのは難しい。
(4)【　】「カントリーロード」は古いヒット曲なので，ジブリが『耳をすませば』で用いるまで日本ではあまり知られていなかった。
(5)【　】ケリーが抱えるいくつもの苦悩は，初期のカントリーミュージシャンたちが抱えた困難を象徴している。

For TOEIC

3．Choose the best answer to complete the sentence.

1．It is difficult for us to understand (　　) the protagonist of this story is happy or not.
　　(A) that　 (B) whether　 (C) why　 (D) how

2．(　　) studio Ghibli had not used it in their animation film in 1995, *Take Me Home, Country Roads* might not be such popular in Japan.
　　(A) Though　 (B) Because　 (C) As　 (D) If

3．(　　) illness, Kelly is forced to live in a rehabilitation facility.
　　(A) Because　 (B) Due to　 (C) Even though　 (D) In spite of

4．(　　) Kelly is a country music superstar, she loses her confidence completely.
　　(A) Although　 (B) However　 (C) But　 (D) Despite

4. Choose the best answer to each question.

1. What will Kelly do after leaving the facility?
    (A) She will get Grammy Award.
    (B) She will manage to accomplish her nationwide tour successfully.
    (C) She will divorce her husband.
    (D) She will hold a concert tour.

2. What is NOT a feature of country music?
    (A) It is translated into many languages.
    (B) It is played with many kinds of instruments.
    (C) It sometimes focuses on the theme of the hardship and poverty of life.
    (D) It is played to an energetic rhythm.

3. When did Olivia Newton-John cover John Denver's song?
    (A) In 1920s
    (B) In 1971
    (C) In 1973
    (D) In 1995

4. What does Shizuku do in *Whisper of the Heart*?
    (A) She gets acquainted with the boy who wants to become a fiddle maker.
    (B) She translates the lyrics of John Denver's old hit song into Japanese.
    (C) She sings an old hit song covered by Olivia Newton-John in English.
    (D) She struggles with her difficulties.

5. Choose the best answer to complete the text.

1. For about a year, she has been forced to live in a rehabilitation facility (1) a nervous breakdown caused by her alcoholism. Kelly got drunk and fell off the stage during a concert.

   (A) due to   (B) because   (C) despite   (D) although

2. Her husband is called James, and he is also her manager. James decides to organize a nationwide concert tour for Kelly. She leaves the rehabilitation facility, even though she has not fully recovered. Her reputation and recovery depend on (2) the tour will be successful or not.

   (A) that   (B) what   (C) how   (D) if

3. The song was covered by Olivia Newton-John two years later, and this cover version became a hit in Japan in 1995, when it featured in the Studio Ghibli animation *Whisper of the Heart*. In that movie, the heroine, Shizuku, translates the lyrics of the song into Japanese and sings the translated version in a memorable scene. (3) this song is quite old, it remains one of the best known, and best loved country songs in Japan.

   (A) In spite of   (B) Because of   (C) Although   (D) However

trivia

　作品の中ですばらしいパフォーマンスをみせたケリー役のグウィネス・パルトロー，ボー役のギャレッド・ヘドランド，チャイルズ役のレイトン・ミースターの3人は，いずれも本業は役者です。一方，ケリーの夫でマネージャーのジェイムズを演じたティム・マックグロウは劇中では一切演奏をすることも歌を歌うこともありませんが，実は名カントリーミュージシャンなのです。

goofs

　ダラスでチャイルズ・スタントンが"A Little Bit Stronger"という歌を歌っているとき，彼女の手はある場面ではお腹のところだったのに，次の場面では胸にあります。

Unit 2
The Grimm Fairy Tales

Vocabulary

1. 本文中に登場する次の (1) ～ (5) の語彙と同じような意味になるものを，下の (a) ～ (e) から選びなさい。

    (1) Traditional animation　　　　　（a）従来のアニメーション
    (2) Cinematography　　　　　　　（b）絵画技法
    (3) Painting techniques　　　　　　（c）映画撮影
    (4) Animation Studious　　　　　　（d）コンピュータグラフィック
    (5) Computer generated imagery　　（e）アニメーションスタジオ

Reading

Tangled is the 50th animated feature film in the Walt Disney Animated Classics series. It was produced in 2010 by Walt Disney Animation Studios. *Tangled* is based on one of the most famous fairy tales in the world, *Rapunzel*. The original tale was collected and published by the 19th century German writers, the Brothers Grimm. The animated movie uses state-of-the-art computer generated imagery (CGI) and 3D cinematography, and stars the voices of Mandy Moore, Donna Murphy, and Zachary Levi.

The movie tells the story of Princess Rapunzel who was stolen from her parents by a witch, Mother Gothel. The witch needs the magical power of Rapunzel's hair to stop herself from growing old. She hides Rapunzel in a tower deep in the forest, and raises her as her own daughter. Gothel constantly tells Rapunzel that the forest is dangerous, and that she must always stay in the tower. One day, a boy, Flynn Rider, discovers the tower, and Rapunzel decides to run away with him to watch dancing lights in the sky and to have other adventures. They run into all kinds of trouble trying to escape Mother Gothel, a band of thieves, and the castle guards.

Tangled quickly became a box office hit. The movie cost about $260 million to make, and in 2010 it was the second most expensive feature film ever produced. The most expensive movie at that time was *The Pirates of the Caribbean: At World's End*. Nevertheless, *Tangled* was very popular, and also very profitable. One of the reasons for its success is a combination of modern CGI and traditional animation painting techniques. By combining the best old techniques with the best new ones, the animation in *Tangled* is smooth, fluid, vibrant, and realistic. While many other animation companies stopped using the traditional painting styles because they were labor intensive and expensive, Disney decided to spend the extra money and were rewarded with excellent reviews from audiences and professional critics.

Walt Disney Animation Studios set a new standard for animated movies with its production of *Tangled*, but the technology alone cannot account for the movie's worldwide popularity. The story idea itself is at least as important as the technology. The *Rapunzel* story is very old, and like all the famous fairy tales, it is a story we have heard many times before. Rapunzel is a "lost child" who is separated from her true family and unaware of her true destiny. Harry Potter is also a "lost child", and so is Luke Skywalker in *StarWars*. Rapunzel's destiny is to become Queen and rescue her kingdom from an "evil force": just like Harry Potter and Luke Skywalker. Ideas like "lost child" and "evil force" are called memes: story elements that are repeated in many different ways. *Tangled* successfully blends some very old story memes with some very new technology, to create a truly beautiful film.

Comprehension Check

2．本文の内容と一致するものには〇，一致しないものには×をつけなさい。
　　（1）【　　】マザー・ゴーテルは良い母になりたかった。
　　（2）【　　】フリン・ライダーは大学で勉強をしたかった。
　　（3）【　　】ラプンツェルは泥棒に怒っています。
　　（4）【　　】良い事は悪より強いです。
　　（5）【　　】森で散歩をすることは身体に良いです。
　　（6）【　　】良い映画を制作するためにはお金をたくさん使わなければいけない。

For TOEIC

3．Choose the best answer to complete the sentence.

1．The story idea itself is at least as important (　　) the technology.
　　（A）so　　（B）than　　（C）as　　（D）with　　（E）even

2．Rapunzel (　　) a "lost child" who is separated from her true family and unaware of her true destiny.
　　（A）was　　（B）are　　（C）has been　　（D）is　　（E）to be

3．The movie tells the story of Princess Rapunzel who was (　　) from her parents by a witch, Mother Gothel.
　　（A）stole　　（B）stolen　　（C）steal　　（D）been　　（E）stealing

4．Tangled quickly (　　) a box office hit.
　　（A）became　　（B）become　　（C）becomes　　（D）was　　（E）did

4. Choose the best answer to each question.

1. Who did write the original story about Rapunzel ?
    (A) Andersen, Hans Christian
    (B) Perrault, Charles
    (C) Brothers Grimm
    (D) Rowling, Joanne K.
    (E) No name

2. Who or what did Rapunzel want to see?
    (A) her parents
    (B) Mother Gothel
    (C) dancing lights
    (D) thieves
    (E) forest

3. What kind of a magic power does Rapunzel have ?
    (A) a magic wand
    (B) a water of life
    (C) a cloak of invisibility
    (D) magic hair
    (E) a ring

4. Which movie was the most expensive one ?
    (A) Tangled
    (B) The Pirates of the Caribbean : At World's End. Nevertheless
    (C) StarWars
    (D) Hobbit
    (E) Cinderella

5. When did the original story publish first ?
    (A) in 2010
    (B) in 20th century
    (C) in the 19th century
    (D) in the 18th century
    (E) the last year

5. Choose the best answer to each question.

1. One day, a boy, Flynn Rider, discovers the tower, and Rapunzel decides to run away with him to watch dancing lights in the sky and to have other adventures. They run (1) all kinds of trouble trying to escape Mother Gothel, a band of thieves, and the castle guards.
   (A) in　(B) to　(C) on　(D) into　(E) at

2. Harry Potter is also a "lost child", and so is Luke Skywalker in *Star Wars*. Rapunzel's destiny is to become Queen and rescue her kingdom from an "evil force": just (2) Harry Potter and Luke Skywalker.
   (A) as　(B) so　(C) like　(D) same　(E) similar

trivia

『タングルド（塔の上のラプンツェル）』は，アメリカ映画協会（MPAA：Motion Picture Association of America）から子どもには親の指導が望ましい映画というPG（Parental Guidance）とされた初めてのディズニーアニメです。

goofs

ラプンツェルとパスカルがかくれんぼをして遊んでいるとき，窓の外には花を描いた絵画がフラワーポットと一緒に映っていますが，後ではその絵画が消えています。

Unit 3
Religious Faith

Vocabulary

1. 本文中に登場する次の(1)〜(7)の語彙と同じような意味になるものを，下の(a)〜(g)から選びなさい。

   (1) Hinduism　　　　　　　　（a）リン光を発する
   (2) botanist　　　　　　　　　（b）ハイエナ
   (3) priest　　　　　　　　　　（c）信　仰
   (4) cargo ship　　　　　　　　（d）ヒンドゥー教
   (5) hyena　　　　　　　　　　（e）司祭，神父
   (6) phosphorescent　　　　　　（f）貨物船
   (7) faith　　　　　　　　　　　（g）植物学者

Reading

Life of Pi is a 2012 film based on Yann Martel's 2001 novel of the same name. The book quickly became a worldwide bestseller, and the film was equally successful. In the film, Pi is an Indian man living in Canada. A writer visits him and asks to hear his life story, because he has heard it is very unusual. Pi tells the writer the story of his childhood in India, about the zoo his father owned, and about his father's decision to sell the zoo and move the whole family to Canada.

Pi describes his childhood search for a religion that suited him. His father did not believe strongly in any religion, he believed in science and medicine. Pi's mother, on the other hand, believed strongly in Hinduism, even though she was a botanist who had studied science her whole life. As a result, Pi did not follow one particular religion as a child, instead he visited all the churches and temples in his town, he talked to all the priests and tried to decide which one was the best.

When the family moves to Canada they travel by cargo ship, because they are selling the animals to a Canadian zoo and need to care for them during the journey. There is a terrible storm and the ship sinks in the Pacific Ocean. Pi manages to get into a lifeboat, but the rest of his family drown. He is shocked and frightened and tries to rescue the animals in his lifeboat. He manages to rescue a hyena, an orangutan, and a zebra, but then he makes the mistake of rescuing a Bengal tiger, and it eats the other animals. So Pi is stranded in the middle of the ocean, in a tiny lifeboat, with a large tiger.

Pi tells the writer many amazing stories about his time in the lifeboat. He sees a whale glowing with phosphorescent plankton, a school of flying fish, and a strange island with trees and meerkats. He survives 227 days at sea before he is rescued by another cargo ship and taken to Canada. The writer doesn't know whether to believe Pi's story or not. Some of the details can be confirmed, like the date of the storm and the date he was rescued, but Pi has no proof that the rest of his story is true.

Life of Pi is an adventure film, but it is also a story about faith. Pi's story is fascinating and many people want to hear it, but the writer points out that he can not confirm anything Pi says, so he must have faith. Pi spent his childhood searching for a religion that suited him, for something he could have faith in, and now it is his own story that requires faith. We never learn if Pi's story is true or not, because faith is part of the story, and faith is only valuable if we have room for doubts.

Comprehension Check

2．本文の内容と一致するものには〇，一致しないものには×をつけなさい。
　（1）【　】パイはインド出身でカナダに住んでいる。
　（2）【　】パイはヒンドゥー教だけを信仰していたが他の宗教も興味があった。
　（3）【　】パイの乗っていた貨物船が難破したとき，救命ボートで助かったのはハイエナとオラウータンとシマウマだけだった。
　（4）【　】パイは227時間漂流して，メキシコのある海岸で助けられた。

For TOEIC

3．Choose the best answer to complete the sentence.

1．A writer visits him and (　　) to hear his life story, because he has heard it is very unusual.
　　（A）ask　（B）asks　（C）asked　（D）had asked

2．When the family moves to Canada they travel (　　) cargo ship
　　（A）to　（B）into　（C）on　（D）by

3．He makes the mistake of (　　) a Bengal tiger.
　　（A）rescue　（B）rescues　（C）rescued　（D）rescuing

4．We never learn (　　) Pi's story is true or not.
　　（A）if　（B）although　（C）though　（D）which

5．Pi manages to (　　) a lifeboat.
　　（A）get into　（B）arrive　（C）save　（D）give

4. Choose the best answer to each question.

1. Who visits him and asks to hear his life story?
    (A) an Indian
    (B) a police officer
    (C) a child
    (D) a writer

2. What did Pi's father believe in?
    (A) He believed in science.
    (B) He believed in medicine.
    (C) He believed in science and medicine.
    (D) He believed in nothing.

3. What was Pi's mother?
    (A) She was a priest.
    (B) She was a writer.
    (C) She was a manager.
    (D) She was a botanist

4. Where are they selling the animals?
    (A) They are selling them to a Canadian zoo.
    (B) They are selling them to an American zoo.
    (C) They are selling them to a Japanese zoo.
    (D) They are selling them to an Indian zoo.

5. Choose the best answer to complete the sentence.

1. *Life of Pi* is a 2012 film based on Yann Martel's 2001 novel of the same name. The book (　　) became a worldwide bestseller, and the film was equally successful
    (A) soon　　(B) always　　(C) now and then　　(D) ordinarily

2. When the family moves to Canada they travel by cargo ship, because they are selling the animals to a Canadian zoo and need to (　　) them during the journey.
    (A) look into　　(B) look before　　(C) look after　　(D) look on

3. He is shocked and frightened and tries to rescue the animals in his lifeboat. He manages to (　　) a hyena, an orangutan, and a zebra.
    (A) help　　(B) save　　(C) give　　(D) leave

trivia

　この映画は，自然の美しさと脅威の双方がとても豊かに表現されています。また，主人公の演技力もとても高く評価されています。
　そこで，もう一つ裏話があります。この物語の監督，台湾出身のアン・リー監督は，初の 3D 作品に挑戦したこの映画で数々の快挙を成し遂げました。そんな，アン・リー監督は，3,000 人を超すオーディションの中から，これが演技初経験というデリー在住の学生スラージ・シャルマを主役に抜擢したのです。さらに，同作にはキャストやクルーとして多くのインド人が参加しているのみならず，ハリウッド映画としては初めて，劇中でインドの豊かな自然や美しい風景が紹介されています。

goofs

　トビウオの集団が去ってしまった後カメラがズームアップしたとき浮き台は消えていましたが，次のシーンでは浮き台がボートにつながれています。

Unit 4
Automaton

Vocabulary

1．本文中に登場する次の(1)～(6)の語彙と同じような意味になるものを，下の(a)～(f)から選びなさい。

(1) invention (a) 魅了，強い関心
(2) automaton (b) 想像力，創作力
(3) signature (c) 発　明
(4) fascination (d) 署　名
(5) audience (e) 機械人形
(6) imagination (f) 聴　衆

Reading

Hugo is an adventure drama film based on Brian Selznick's 2007 novel *The Invention of Hugo Cabret*. The film was released in 2011, and stars Asa Butterfield as Hugo. Martin Scorsese directed the film and it was his first 3D movie. In 2012, *Hugo* was nominated for eleven Academy Awards (unofficially called "Oscars"), and it won five of them. *Hugo* tells the story of a young boy who is fascinated by the works of an old film maker named Georges Méliès.

Hugo Cabret is a young boy who lives in Paris during the 1930s. His father, a film fanatic and amateur inventor, was killed in a museum fire. Since his father's death, Hugo has lived in the walls of the Paris Gare Montparnasse railway station, where he maintains all the station clocks. His father was building a mechanical man, an automaton, when he died, and Hugo often reads his father's notes and tries to complete the automaton on his own. One day, a toy maker catches Hugo stealing from his shop. He fights with Hugo, finds the notes about the automaton, and offers to help Hugo finish it, in return for Hugo working in the shop. The toy maker, Papa Georges, has an adopted daughter called Isabelle who becomes close friends with Hugo. Eventually, the automaton is finished, but it doesn't work because it needs a heart-shaped key to wind it up. Hugo notices that Isabelle wears a heart-shaped key on a necklace, and when they try it in the automaton, it fits perfectly. They wind up the automaton and it begins to move. It looks like it is drawing a picture, so Hugo puts a pencil in its hand and a piece of paper on the table. The automaton draws a famous scene from one of Georges Méliès's films, and then signs his name at the bottom. Isabelle recognizes the signature, it is Papa Georges's. He is really a famous film maker.

The automaton in this film is based on the wind-up dolls which were popular in Europe during the 18th Century. The name "automaton" comes from the Ancient Greek word *auto* which means "self". Words with *auto* in them usually mean things that happen on their own, such as *automatic* washing machines, *automobile* engines. The 18th Century automatons were usually designed and built by watchmakers and clock smiths, because they required tiny gears and delicate parts. A famous automaton was a mechanical duck made by the French inventor, Jaques de Vaucanson in 1753. The duck flapped its wings, drank water, and sang. Many people were fascinated by the wind-up duck, and it inspired more engineers to design better, more powerful machines.

Hugo is a fantasy adventure story, but the characters' fascination with mechanics and automation were very real. The movie is set in a time before digital technology and computer-assisted design. The films Hugo loves have no special effects, and the automaton he is building does not run on electricity. One of the reasons this film is so popular is that audiences are impressed with the imagination and skills of the old watchmakers and clock smiths who could design and build such beautiful machines without the help of computers.

Comprehension Check

2．本文の内容と一致するものには〇，一致しないものには×をつけなさい。
　　（1）【　　】この映画は小説を元に制作された映画である。
　　（2）【　　】ヒューゴが持っていたメモはメリエスが書いたものである。
　　（3）【　　】機械人形を動かす鍵はイザベルが持っていた。
　　（4）【　　】イザベルはジョルジュ・メリエスの養女である。
　　（5）【　　】ぜんまい仕掛けのアヒルはフランスの時計職人によって製作された。

For TOEIC

3．Choose the best answer to complete the sentence.

1．When I came home, my wife (　　　) a book in the living room.
　　(A) reads　　(B) is reading　　(C) has read　　(D) was reading

2．He (　　) be hungry, for he has just eaten hamburgers.
　　(A) can't　　(B) may　　(C) must　　(D) oughtn't

3．I was surprised (　　　) the news.
　　(A) at　　(B) to　　(C) in　　(D) by

4．On my way home, I was (　　　) a stranger.
　　(A) spoken by　　(B) spoken to by　　(C) spoken at　　(D) spoken with by

5．(　　　) boy loves to play soccer.
　　(A) Many　　(B) All the　　(C) Every　　(D) Most of the

4. Choose the best answer to each question.

1. What is this movie about?
   (A) History of France
   (B) An automaton and a movie maker
   (C) Automobile technology
   (D) Station clocks

2. When was *The Invention of Hugo Cabret* released?
   (A) in 1930
   (B) in 2007
   (C) in 2011
   (D) in 2012

3. Why did Hugo live in the walls of a railway station?
   (A) to build automaton
   (B) because he was a homeless orphan
   (C) to read his father's notes
   (D) because he wanted to keep the station clock accurate

4. What made the automaton work?
   (A) The station clock
   (B) Hugo's father's notes
   (C) A key which is shaped like a heart
   (D) A strong wind

5. Who made the wind-up duck?
   (A) Hugo
   (B) Jaques de Vaucanson
   (C) Ancient Greek
   (D) Georges Méliès

5. Choose the best answer to each question.

1. His father was building a mechanical man, an automaton, when he died, and Hugo often reads his father's notes and tries to complete the automaton (　　).
   (A) quickly　(B) with ease　(C) without any tools　(D) by himself

2. The automation draws a famous scene from one of Georges Méliès's films, and then signs his name at the bottom. Isabelle (　　) the signature. It is Papa Georges's.
   (A) recognizes　(B) writes　(C) understands　(D) represents

3. (　　) people were fascinated by the wind-up duck, and it inspired more engineers to design better, more powerful machines.
   (A) A number of　(B) The number of　(C) A few　(D) Few

trivia

　映画のタイトルは当初，原作の原題『The Invention of Hugo Cabret』でしたが，『Hugo Cabret』と呼ばれ，のちにさらに縮められて『Hugo』となりました。

Goofs

　イザベラがヒューゴに鍵を手渡した場面で（49分頃），二人の間に機械人形が見えるのですが，機械人形はペンを握っていません。ヒューゴもイザベラもペンを取り付けていないのに，ヒューゴが鍵を回したとき，人形はすでにペンを握って書き出そうとしています。

Unit 5
Environmental Problem

Vocabulary

1. 本文中に登場する次の(1)～(6)の語彙と同じような意味になるものを，下の(a)～(f)から選びなさい。

(1) environment　　　　　　　（a）検　査
(2) experiment　　　　　　　 （b）保　護
(3) protection　　　　　　　　（c）環　境
(4) consumption　　　　　　　（d）消　費
(5) earthquake　　　　　　　　（e）地　震
(6) inspection　　　　　　　　 （f）実　験

Reading

    No Impact Man is a documentary film telling the story of a New York family who try to live without making any impact on the environment. Colin Beavan is an author, and his wife, Michelle, is a journalist. They live in Manhattan with their daughter, Isabella, who is two years old. Together, they have a comfortable, wealthy lifestyle, but Colin is unhappy
5 about the damage their lifestyle is doing to the environment. He decides to conduct a year-long experiment : they will try to find a lifestyle that makes no negative impact on the environment.

    Their first goal was to stop creating trash. This was difficult because it meant they could not buy anything that had packaging, no paper towels, no Starbucks coffee, no
10 shopping bags. Next, they tried to live without electricity : no lights, no air-conditioning, no television. Then they tried to buy only food that was produced within 250 miles of New York : no fruit from Africa, no coffee or chocolate from South America. Finally, they tried to stop polluting the air and water : no chemical detergents, no gasoline cars, no fossil fuels.

15   We have all heard about the "4Rs" of environmental protection : Reduce, Reuse, Repair Recycle. The Beavan family lived that way for a year. They still lived in their Manhattan apartment, but they reduced their consumption of fossil fuels by taking the stairs instead of the elevator. They used candles instead of electric lights, and they didn't turn on the air-conditioner. They reused old cloth as toilet paper and used reusable cups
20 instead of disposable paper ones. They didn't buy anything new for the whole year, so whenever something broke, they had no choice but to repair it. Finally, they recycled as much of their garbage as possible. They started a worm farm and used it to dispose of all their organic waste instead of putting it in the trash.

    The Beavans learned a lot during their no impact year. They learned about where
25 food comes from and how much energy is consumed to produce it and transport it around the world. They learned to cook meals using local food and as little energy as possible. They learned to be less dependent on cars and more dependent on walking and cycling to travel around the city. They all lost weight and became much healthier. Their hair and skin looked and felt much better when they stopped using chemical soaps and shampoos.
30   *No Impact Man* was released in 2009, and in 2011 Japan experienced a devastating earthquake and tsunami. As well as destroying homes, farms, and transport networks, the tsunami also caused a nuclear disaster at the Fukushima Daiichi Nuclear Power Station. Vast quantities of radiation contaminated the air, water, and soil for many kilometers around the disaster site. Also, all of Japan's nuclear power stations had to be
35 switched off for safety inspections. Suddenly, everybody in Japan was forced to think

about living a lifestyle with less energy, locally-produced food, and less consumption of natural resources. The *No Impact Man* project has many important lessons for modern Japan and the rest of the world.

Comprehension Check

2．本文の内容と一致するものには○，一致しないものには×をつけなさい。
　　（1）【　】映画 *No Impact Man* は，実話を元にしている。
　　（2）【　】ビーヴァン夫妻は自分で作った野菜しか食べない。
　　（3）【　】ビーヴァン夫妻はトイレットペーパーとして古新聞を利用する。
　　（4）【　】映画 *No Impact Man* が封切られる直前に，日本で大地震が起こった。

For TOEIC

3．Choose the best answer to complete the sentence.

1．If they had not started the *No Impact Man* Project, they (　　) the value of the natural resources.
　　（A）could not have realized　　（B）didn't realize
　　（C）don't realize　　（D）could not realizing

2．They buy neither coffee, (　　) chocolate
　　（A）and　　（B）so　　（C）not　　（D）nor

3．Colin has changed his life into a more (　　) one
　　（A）satisfy　　（B）satisfied　　（C）being satisfied　　（D）satisfying

4．The air, (　　) they breathe in New York, is contaminated.
　　（A）what　　（B）where　　（C）which　　（D）whose

4. Choose the best answer to each question.

1. What is Colin Beavan's job?
    (A) He is an author.
    (B) He is a journalist.
    (C) He has no job.
    (D) He is a cameraman.

2. Why was it difficult for the Beavan family to stop creating trash?
    (A) Because they were not able to buy anything that had no packaging.
    (B) Because they lived in an apartment.
    (C) Because they don't know how to recycle what they would buy.
    (D) Because most of the food which they would buy was not produced within 250 miles of New York.

3. When was *No Impact Man* released?
    (A) In 2011.
    (B) In 2009.
    (C) Just after the big earthquake in Japan.
    (D) Just after the nuclear disaster in Japan.

4. What did the Beavan family keep in order to dispose of their organic waste?
    (A) ducks
    (B) a dog
    (C) worms
    (D) fish

5. Choose the best answer to complete the sentence.

1. Whenever something broke, they (　　) repair it.
　　(A) were forced to　　(B) were grateful to
　　(C) afforded to　　(D) subscribed to

2. Their first (　　) was to stop creating trash.
　　(A) tone　(B) manner　(C) aim　(D) description

trivia

　映画の中では，ミッシェルが環境にやさしい生活をする一方で，資本主義の旗振り役である「ビジネスウィーク」に勤務していることを批判されていました。一方で「ビジネスウィーク」の経営者であるマイケル・ブルームバーグは歴代で最も人気の高いニューヨーク市長であり，在任中に大手清涼飲料メーカーの反対を押し切り，ファーストフードなどの飲食店や映画館において炭酸飲料のLサイズの提供を禁止しています（係争中）。

goofs

　この映画は，台本に従って撮影される映画とは異なり，（やらせ作品ではない）ドキュメンタリーであり登場人物の失敗はあってもgoofsは存在しません。しかし，一方で観客がツッコミを入れたくなるような場面はあります。たとえば，電気を消費する冷蔵庫は使えないために，野菜の保冷に苦労してしまい，知人に氷をもらって代用するという場面があります。

Unit 6
Asian Disciple to Reach Maturity

Vocabulary

1. 本文中に登場する次の(1)～(5)の語彙と同じような意味になるものを，下の(a)～(e)から選びなさい。

   (1) star   (a) 暴　力
   (2) move   (b) 哲　学
   (3) martial arts (c) 武　術
   (4) philosophy   (d) 引っ越す
   (5) violence   (e) 主演する

Reading

The Karate Kid is a 2010 re-boot of a 1984 movie of the same name. The 1984 movie starred Ralph Macchio and Pat Morita, and the 2010 movie stars Jaden Smith and Jackie Chan. Both movies tell the story of a young boy who is forced to move to a new city and attend a new school. After being bullied by a local gang of martial arts students, the boy finds a teacher to help with his problems. The boy learns to fight, but he also learns about the philosophy of not fighting, of dealing with problems without turning to violence.

In *The Karate Kid* (2010), 12 year-old Dre Parker moves from Detroit to Beijing because his mother finds a job there. Dre is bullied and beaten-up by a gang of boys who are all students at a kung-fu school. During a fight, he is rescued by Mr. Han, the maintenance man in Dre's apartment building. Mr. Han is a kung-fu master and Dre begs him to teach him how to fight. Mr. Han is reluctant to teach Dre because he thinks his training will result in Dre getting into even more fights. Eventually, Mr. Han realizes that the bullies won't leave Dre alone, and he finally agrees to train him in kung-fu.

Although Mr. Han knows that Dre wants to learn kung-fu because he intends to fight with the bullies, he is concerned that Dre might become a good fighter, and then become a bully himself. He tries to teach Dre about the philosophy of kung-fu, about controlling his anger and remaining peaceful no matter what other people do to him. They visit a kung-fu temple and watch a woman standing face-to-face with a snake. At first Dre thinks the woman is mirroring the snake's movements, but he soon realizes the opposite is true : the snake is mirroring the woman's movements. Mr. Han explains that it would be impossible to force the snake to copy the woman's movements, but because she is peaceful and confident, she can lead the snake to do what she does. Dre learns that peaceful leadership is more effective than aggressive force.

Of course, at the end of the movie Dre must face the gang of bullies. They meet in a kung-fu competition, and Dre is forced to fight many rounds to meet the leader of the gang, Cheng. Although Dre is hurt, frightened, and angry, he remembers Mr. Han's lessons and he is able to stay peaceful and confident throughout the fight. Cheng, on the other hand, is full of anger and hatred, so he fights recklessly. Dre is able to defeat Cheng and win the competition, and the rest of the gang is forced to leave him alone.

Mr. Han teaches Dre some important lessons about kung-fu, fighting, and overcoming fear. But his lessons are not limited to martial arts. If we can remain peaceful in dangerous or frightening situations, we can find solutions to our problems. If we can be confident without being aggressive or forceful, we can lead others to behave the way we do.

Comprehension Check

2．本文の内容と一致するものには〇，一致しないものには×をつけなさい。
　（1）【　】1984年の『カラテキッド』は，2010年のそれとは違う作品です。
　（2）【　】『カラテキッド』で，主人公は父親の転勤でデトロイトに引っ越します。
　（3）【　】ドレの師匠のハン氏はカラテ学校の先生です。
　（4）【　】ハン氏は，平穏でいることは大事だが怒りを持つことも大事だと教えます。

For TOEIC

3．Choose the best answer to complete the sentence.

（1）The 1984 movie (　　) Ralph Macchio and Pat Morita
　　（a）starred　（b）star　（c）starring　（d）stars

（2）Two movies both tell the story of a young boy (　　) is forced to move to a new city.
　　（a）which　（b）who　（c）when　（d）where

（3）In *The Karate Kid*, Dre begs Mr. Han to teach him (　　) to fight.
　　（a）what　（b）which　（c）how　（d）so

（4）The woman can lead the snake to do (　　) she does, because she is peaceful.
　　（a）which　（b）enough　（c）where　（d）what

4. Choose the best answer to each question.

1. What is this movie about?
    (A) Horror Movie
    (B) Human Drama
    (C) Science Fiction
    (D) Love Comedy

2. What does Mr. Han do in daily life?
    (A) A maintenance man
    (B) A Karate teacher
    (C) A movie star
    (D) A poilceman

3. Why does Dre want to learn kung-fu?
    (A) Because he wants to help someone.
    (B) Because he wants to become a movie star.
    (C) Because he wants to make a lot of money.
    (D) Because he wants to beat local martial arts students.

5. Choose the best answer to each question.

1. Mr. Han is (   ) to teach Dre because he thinks his training will result in Dre getting into even more fights.
    (A) going   (B) eager   (C) free   (D) unwilling

2. Dre remembers Mr. Han's lessons and he (   ) stay peaceful and confident throughout the fight.
    (A) must   (B) can   (C) may   (D) shall

trivia

　映画でDreの誕生日が壁に記されている場面があります。この誕生日，Dre役を演じているJaden Smithの実際の誕生日なのです。また，Han（Jackie Chan）からもらったシャツを見てDreが「Bruce Leeの服みたい」と言う場面がありますが，実はJackieとBruce Leeは映画で共演しています。JackieはBruce主演の映画 Enter the Dragon：邦題『燃えよドラゴン』（1973）にチョイ役（悪役）で出演し，Bruceに一瞬にして倒されています。

goofs

　ミスター・ハンの事務所で彼はドレ・パーカーに水がいっぱいに入ったグラスを与えますが，ドレが傾けたグラスは空でした。

Asian Disciple to Reach Maturity

Unit 7
Bioengineering and Society

Vocabulary

1. 本文中に登場する次の(1)～(6)の語句の意味として最も適切なものを，(a)～(f)の中から1つずつ選びなさい。

   (1) experiment　　　　　　（a）根絶する
   (2) transform　　　　　　（b）難　聴
   (3) blindness　　　　　　（c）変形させる
   (4) deafness　　　　　　（d）移植する
   (5) eradicate　　　　　　（e）実験する
   (6) transplant　　　　　　（f）失　明

Reading

  The Amazing Spider-Man is a re-boot of the classic *Spider-Man* story that was first published as a comic book in 1962. The movie was released in 2012 and stars Andrew Garfield as Peter Parker. *Spider-Man* continues to appear in comic books, as well as in movies, animations, and even theme parks.

  The movie follows the story of Peter Parker. He is a high school student who lives with his aunt and uncle because his parents disappeared when he was very young. Peter learns that his parents were scientists and that they worked at a large company called Oscorp. He visits the laboratory at Oscorp to investigate their disappearance, and he is bitten by a genetically-modified spider.

  The spider is part of an experiment by Dr. Connors. He has only one arm and he has been researching ways to grow new limbs. He has been experimenting with lizard DNA. In spite of the danger, he tests his new drug on himself. He grows a new arm, but the drug is too powerful and Dr. Connors is transformed into a giant lizard monster. Lizard causes panic and chaos as he goes around New York and nothing seems to be able to stop him. However, Peter's spider bite is also transforming him. He develops super-human strength. He can climb walls and spin webs just like a spider. He can see and hear much better than a normal human, so he goes looking for Lizard, to try and stop him. Lizard and Spider-Man fight on the Williamsburg Bridge, and eventually Spider-Man wins, and saves the people on the bridge.

  The Amazing Spider-Man is a fantasy story, but it makes us think about genetic engineering. Many scientists are researching genetic engineering to find ways to help humans. They are researching ways to cure disabilities like blindness and deafness. They are researching ways to repair damaged organs such as hearts and lungs. They are researching ways to eradicate diseases such as malaria and AIDS. There is no doubt that their intentions are good and that their goal is to make the world safer and healthier. However, some people are concerned that the scientists are moving too quickly. They believe that too little time is spent planning and evaluating genetic experiments. While nobody really believes that scientists will accidentally make a lizard monster, some people worry that small mistakes might have very serious consequences in the future.

  In Japan, scientists like Dr. Shinya Yamanaka are researching technologies to improve the lives of people with disabilities. In 2012 Dr. Yamanaka won the Nobel Prize for Physiology or Medicine for his research into iPS cells, which scientists hope may eventually be used for repairing damaged organs. In the future, these cells may be able to grow new organs, such as a heart or a kidney. This means that people will be able to have transplant organs that are perfectly matched to their own DNA. The fantasies about genetic engineering might be scary, and we may want superheroes like Spider-Man to save us, but in reality, it is scientists like Dr. Yamanaka who are the real heroes, and who will save people in real life.

Comprehension Check

2．本文の内容と一致するものには〇，一致しないものには×をつけなさい。
　　（1）【　　】『スパイダーマン』は映画だけでなく，漫画やアニメも製作されている。
　　（2）【　　】Peter Parker は高校を卒業して，科学者として Oscorp 社で働いている。
　　（3）【　　】Dr. Connors は片腕がなく，新しい腕を再生させる実験を行っている。
　　（4）【　　】遺伝子工学は臓器の修復や難病の治療など人間の生命にも関わっている。

For TOEIC

3．Choose the best answer to complete the sentence.

1．The *Spider-Man* story (　　) as a comic book in 1962.
　　（A）will publish　　（B）published
　　（C）was published　　（D）was publishing

2．Peter has lived with his aunt and uncle (　　) his parents disappeared.
　　（A）unless　　（B）since　　（C）however　　（D）if

3．(　　) the danger, Dr. Connors tests his new drug on himself.
　　（A）In spite of　　（B）Because of　　（C）Instead of　　（D）Due to

4．Peter can see and hear much (　　) than a normal human.
　　（A）well　　（B）clearly　　（C）best　　（D）better

5．Scientists hope iPS cells will be used for (　　) damaged organs.
　　（A）repairing　　（B）repaired
　　（C）being repaired　　（D）been repaired

4. Choose the best answer to each question.

1. What does Spider-Man do in daily life ?
    (A) A high school student
    (B) A teacher
    (C) A movie star
    (D) An engineer

2. Why does Peter visit the laboratory at Oscorp ?
    (A) To have a job interview
    (B) To research ways to grow new limbs
    (C) To experiment with lizard DVA
    (D) To get information about his parents

3. How did Dr. Connors turn into Lizard ?
    (A) He was bit by a spider.
    (B) He injected a drug into his arm.
    (C) He took a powerful medicine.
    (D) He fought against a large monster.

4. What is Not mentioned about Dr. Shinya Yamanaka ?
    (A) He received the Nobel Prize for Physiology or Medicine.
    (B) His research can lead to the improvement of damaged organs.
    (C) He is one of the scientists who will be able to save people.
    (D) He is a big fan of *Spider-Man* and enjoys watching the movie.

5. Choose the best answer to complete the text.

  The Amazing Spider-Man is a fantasy story, but it makes us think about genetic engineering. Many scientists are researching genetic engineering to find out （　1　） to help humans. There is no doubt that their intentions are good and that their goal is to make the world safer and healthier. However, some people are （　2　） that the scientists are moving too quickly. They believe that too little time is spent planning and evaluating genetic experiments. （　3　） nobody really believes that scientists will accidentally make a lizard monster, some people worry that small mistakes might have very serious consequences in the future.

  （1）（A）who　（B）when　（C）where　（D）how
  （2）（A）positive　（B）eager　（C）afraid　（D）curious
  （3）（A）Therefore　（B）Although　（C）Also　（D）Despite

trivia

　本映画において，ステーシー警部はスパイダーマンの行動に強く反対し（最終的に警部は自分が間違っていたと認めるけれども），グウェンはスパイダーマンとしてのピーターの役割に気づき，支持的な態度を示します。映画でのこうした点は，コミックシリーズとは著しい対照をなしています。コミックにおいては，ステーシー警部はスパイダーマンの支持者で，死に際にピーターの正体に気づいていたことを打ち明けます。その一方で，グウェンは父親（警部）の死をスパイダーマンのせいにし，ピーターはグウェンに自分の正体を一度も知らせないでいます。

goofs

　映画の終わりの方で，グウェンがオズコープタワーを出て，歩道にいるステーシー警部に会いに行く場面があります。警部の車が急ブレーキをかける音が聞こえるのですが，車はそのシーンの始めから，ドアが開いた状態ですでに止まっています。

Unit 8
Complex and Pride

Vocabulary

1. 本文中に登場する次の (1) 〜 (5) の語彙と同じような意味になるものを，下の (a) 〜 (e) から選びなさい。

    (1) charismatic　　　　　　　（a）直面する
    (2) vulgar　　　　　　　　　（b）乱暴な
    (3) be inferior to　　　　　　（c）公　務
    (4) face　　　　　　　　　　（d）〜より劣る
    (5) public duties　　　　　　（e）カリスマ性

Reading

The King's Speech is a 2010 drama starring Colin Firth and Geoffrey Rush. It follows the story of Prince Albert trying to overcome his fear of public speaking so that he will be able to perform his public duties when he becomes king. The story takes place in England in 1925. Prince Albert is the second son of King George V. His father is very strong and strict, so Prince Albert is afraid of him. His older brother is very confident and charismatic, so Prince Albert is intimidated by him. Prince Albert feels inferior to both his father and his brother, and this causes him a lot of stress. As a result of this stress, Prince Albert has a severe stammer. Talking privately is difficult for him, and public speaking is impossible.

Prince Albert asks many doctors for their advice to help him stop stammering. In the movie we see him smoking cigarettes, drinking strong brandy, and filling his mouth with glass marbles. The treatments look funny, but none of them are effective, and Prince Albert still stammers. Finally, his wife talks to an Australian speech therapist who promises to help him. Lionel Logue refuses to travel to Buckingham Palace, and he refuses to call Prince Albert "Your Royal Highness", and he insists on treating Prince Albert's stammer with his own strange methods. Logue calls Prince Albert by his family's nickname, "Bertie", and encourages him to be angry, to use vulgar language, to shout, to roll around on the floor ; all the things a prince is not supposed to do. Eventually after his father's death and his brother's abdication, Prince Albert becomes King George VI and he has to face his new public duties.

The new King is terrified because he has to make a speech at his coronation. Hundreds of people will be watching his coronation ceremony, and millions of people will listen to his speech on the radio. King George VI once again asks Logue to help him overcome his fears. Logue continues to call him "Bertie", and during their private meetings they shout, swear, and jump around, so that the King can relax enough to speak clearly. With Logue's help the King is able to make his coronation speech. He also makes regular public speeches and radio broadcasts with Logue's help and encouragement. When World War II begins, Logue stands beside him and helps him through the most difficult speech so far : announcing to the British public that they are now at war with Germany.

The King's Speech makes us think about how stress and anxiety affect us in our daily lives. Everybody experiences anxiety, even princes and kings, and we all have to learn how to deal with our problems. In the movie, King George VI overcomes his anxiety by asking for help. He learns that anxiety problems cannot solve themselves and that he must work hard to achieve his goals. In the end he realizes that he is not inferior to his father or his older brother. He learns that he can be strong and earnest and perform his public duties without fear or anxiety.

Comprehension Check

2．本文の内容と一致するものには○，一致しないものには×をつけなさい。
　（1）【　】ジョージ5世は剛健で厳しい王であったので，アルバート公と彼の兄はひどい吃音になった。
　（2）【　】アルバート公の妻は彼を助けるために，ローグにその支援を求めた。
　（3）【　】戴冠式の直前に，ローグの指導を受けたジョージ6世は無事に演説をすることができた。
　（4）【　】誰もが不安や問題を抱えているのが現実で，それを克服するためには静観しなければならない。

For TOEIC

3．Choose the best answer to complete the sentences.

1．This is the park (　　) I used to take a walk every morning.
　　(A) that　　(B) which　　(C) what　　(D) where

2．She will be glad to see you when she (　　) home.
　　(A) comes　　(B) will come　　(C) coming　　(D) came

3．I don't know if she (　　) back next spring.
　　(A) will come　　(B) coming　　(C) came　　(D) comes

4．(　　) Japanese like to eat rice.
　　(A) Most of　　(B) Almost　　(C) Almost of　　(D) Almost all

5．It is time you (　　) to bed.
　　(A) gone　　(B) going　　(C) went　　(D) to go

4．Choose the best answer to each question.

1．What is the movie about？
（A）How to study stress
（B）How to escape from stress
（C）How to like stress
（D）How to deal with stress

2．What advice did many doctors give Prince Albert？
（A）To fill his mouth with glass marbles
（B）To smoke cigarettes
（C）To dance beautifully
（D）To drink strong brandy

3．What was Logue's strange method？
（A）To run around
（B）To smoke much
（C）To announce with smile
（D）To use rough words

4．Who was called "Bertie"？
（A）King George V
（B）His older brother
（C）King George VI
（D）Lionel Logue

5. Choose the best answer to complete the sentence.

1. As a (　　) of this stress, Prince Albert has a severe stammer. Talking privately is difficult for him, and public speaking is impossible.
   (A) because　(B) order　(C) according　(D) consequence

2. It follows the story of Prince Albert trying to overcome his fear of public speaking (　　) he will be able to perform his public duties when he becomes king.
   (A) as　(B) since　(C) so　(D) because of

trivia

　1970年半ば頃まで，ビー玉は子どもたちにとってなくてはならないものでした。ビー玉の美しさとそのゲームの面白さを追い求めて，かなり熱くなったことを覚えています。たとえば，三角出し（現代ならカーリングに似ている），穴入れ（ゴルフのパターぽい），目落としや線引きなどいろいろあったことを覚えています。しかし，1970年代末から，インベーダーゲームが出現し，その後，80年代はファミコンが日本中の子どもたちを虜にしてしまった。それ以降，パソコンゲームが主流となり，いつしかビー玉は消えていきました。ビー玉は，映画の世界では，言語矯正の手段として使用されていましたが，実際の世界では，リハビリでの機能回復のため，また足裏などの刺激のために使用されています。ファッションとしては，アクセサリーや手水鉢の美飾に扱われています。ビー玉の歴史はかなり古いとされています。時代によって，その使用目的が変遷したのは想像つきますが，果たして日本の子どもたちをあれほど楽しませた時代と地域が他にあったのかと考えてしまいます。いつか，ビー玉は新たなスタイルで進化して再ブレークすることを願っています。

goofs

　英国王ジョージ6世は午後6時にスピーチを始めたのに，時計は午後7時20分を示しています。

Unit 9
Major League Baseball

Vocabulary

1. 本文中に登場する次の(1)～(7)の語彙と同じような意味になるものを，下の(a)～(g)から選びなさい。

（1）lucrative　　　　（a）奮闘する
（2）contract　　　　（b）契　約
（3）diploma　　　　（c）説得する
（4）struggle　　　　（d）卒業証書
（5）effective　　　　（e）優　先
（6）priority　　　　（f）効果的な
（7）persuade　　　　（g）もうかる

Reading

Major League Baseball is a big business in the United States of America. The best players from all over the world are drawn to the Major League to play for some of the best teams in the world. Baseball is one of the most popular sports in America and it is a very lucrative business for both the players and the owners of the teams. The teams
5 spend tremendous amounts of money to buy talented players who can help them win the championships. *Moneyball* is a 2011 movie, starring Brad Pitt, which follows the story of a baseball scout trying to build a winning team.

Scouting baseball players begins while they are still very young. Professional scouts attend high school baseball games and look out for young players who have a lot of talent.
10 Some of these teenagers have to make difficult decisions about their lives while they are still in school. For example, they may have to choose between signing a lucrative contract with a baseball team and going to college. In *Moneyball*, Billy Beane chose a baseball career because the contract was worth a lot of money. The contract meant that Billy could not go to college because he had to train with the team every day. In the beginning,
15 Billy enjoys all the money and attention, but his baseball skills are not so great, and he retires at a young age.

Billy has no education except for his high school diploma so he goes to work for the Oakland Athletics baseball team. Although the Athletics are a Major League team, they do not rank very highly and therefore are not as rich as many of the other teams. Billy
20 struggles to buy talented players when the other teams can offer so much more money. When he meets Peter Brand, an economics graduate, they develop a new system for choosing young players. The other Oakland Athletics managers and scouts do not support the new system, so Billy and Peter have to struggle to test their system properly. Eventually, they are able to draft a team of young players who have been ignored by the
25 other teams, but who rank highly according to the new system. The Athletics win the championship and everyone is forced to accept that the new system is effective.

Following the success of Billy's drafting system, the Boston Red Sox try to headhunt him to lead their drafting team. The Red Sox are one of the most famous Major League teams, and they offer Billy over 12 million dollars to join their team. Billy remembers the
30 decision he made in high school when he chose a lucrative contract over his own education. This time he decides that money is not his priority and he turns down the Red Sox's offer.

Moneyball gives us a look at what happens behind the scenes in Major League Baseball. We can see how many young players are persuaded to leave school and how
35 much money is spent "gambling" on who the future stars will be. More importantly, we

can see how many talented players never get the chance to perform, and also how many players are forced to quit early because their performance is not as good as hoped. Most importantly, we can see how important is to think carefully about life decisions, to consider our happiness as well as our money.

Comprehension Check

2．本文の内容と一致するものには○，一致しないものには×をつけなさい。
   （1）【　】メジャーリーグの選手たちは全員アメリカ人である。
   （2）【　】アメリカでは大学進学かプロに進むかという難しい選択を迫られる高校球児たちがいる。
   （3）【　】ビリーは大学を卒業後，オークランドアスレチックスに入団した。
   （4）【　】ビリーは仕事のことでピーターとうまくやっていけなかった。
   （5）【　】ビリーはレッドソックスから高額の年俸を提示されたが入団を断った。

For TOEIC

3．Choose the best answer to each question.

1．Oakland is a city (　　) Billy worked as the general manager of a professional baseball team.
   （A）who　（B）which　（C）where　（D）when

2．(　　) by the fans and other executives of the team, Billy tried very hard with Peter to find a way the Athletics could win the pennant.
   （A）Criticizing　（B）To criticize　（C）Criticism　（D）Criticized

3．He could not (　　) along with his coworkers because he never listened to their opinions and grievances.
   （A）get　（B）take　（C）keep　（D）come

4．It is not (　　) true that young players who have a lot of talent can be successful in their careers.
   （A）necessary　（B）necessarily　（C）necessity　（D）necessitate

5. The Athletics struggled to buy talented players because they were on a (　　) budget.
   (A) lean   (B) tremendous   (C) profitable   (D) proper

4. Choose the best answer to each question.

1. Why do professional scouts come to see high-school baseball games?
   (A) Because they are interested in sports.
   (B) Because they need to see the managers.
   (C) Because they want to find good players.
   (D) Because they have to sign the contract.

2. What did Billy become after graduating from high school?
   (A) A college student
   (B) A manager
   (C) A baseball player
   (D) A movie star

3. What did Peter major in at college?
   (A) Business
   (B) Baseball
   (C) System Engineering
   (D) Economics

4. When did the Red Sox try to headhunt Billy?
   (A) After the Oakland Athletics won the championship.
   (B) When Billy developed a new system for choosing young players.
   (C) When Billy decided to sign a lucrative contract.
   (D) While he was a professional baseball player.

5. Choose the best answer to each question.

  The National Pastime. That's what baseball is called in America. Baseball players keep practicing every day and putting in serious efforts to win the games, but winning is not the one and only purpose for (1) they play baseball. Both baseball players and fans think that they have to enjoy themselves by playing and watching the games. Many (2) enjoy chatting with their friends over a glass of beer or rooting for their home team. People in the ballpark share the time with each other and find baseball fun and (3).

  (1) (A) that (B) which (C) what (D) when
  (2) (A) guests (B) customers (C) clients (D) spectators
  (3) (A) enjoying (B) enjoy (C) enjoyable (D) to enjoy

trivia

　ビリーの娘ケイシーが自分が作った歌として楽器店の中でビリーに歌って聞かせる歌は，実は，オーストラリア出身の歌手 Lenka が 2008 年にリリースした「The Show」という曲が元歌になっています。映画の最後のシーンで再度この歌が流れますが，そこでは You're such a loser, dad... Just enjoy the show. というオリジナルとは異なる歌詞になっています。ビリーはＧＭ（general manager）としてその素晴らしい手腕を発揮し，好成績を収めるにもかかわらず，最後の試合で負けてしまいます。しかし，自分のロジックをあくまでも貫き通すという彼の生きざまをこの歌詞が象徴しているように思えます。また，ビリーのブレーンとして活躍するピーター・ブランドは，映画の中ではメリーランド州出身，イエール大学卒業の秀才ですが，モデルになった実際の人物はポール・デポデスタという名前で，バージニア州出身，ハーバード大学卒業です。映画に登場するようなメタボな体つきではなく，どちらかというとすらっとした体格の男性です。

goofs

　この映画は，2002 年のシーズンを舞台にしたものですが，映画の終盤，ビリーがレッドソックスの本拠地，フェンウェイパークを訪れるとき，バックネット上のプレスルームの壁に 2004 年と 2007 年のワールドシリーズ優勝フラッグが掲げてあるのが見えます。また，中央の内野 2 〜 3 階席が見えていますが，2002 年当時，そこには 406 クラブという大型ガラス張りのセクションがあり，それが取り払われたのは 2005 年のことです。レフト側の高いフェンス（グリーンモンスター）の上に見える客席も，実は 2003 年に増築されたもので，2002 年にはまだ存在していません。

Unit 10
Business

Vocabulary

1．本文中に登場する次の (1) 〜 (5) の語彙と同じような意味になるものを，下の (a) 〜 (e) から選びなさい。

（1）divert　　　　　　　　　（a）薄める
（2）controversial　　　　　　（b）転換する
（3）stall　　　　　　　　　　（c）買　収
（4）dilute　　　　　　　　　（d）先延ばしする
（5）asset　　　　　　　　　　（e）財　産
（6）acquisition　　　　　　　（f）自律性
（7）autonomy　　　　　　　　（g）物議を醸す

Reading

  In 2004, a new social networking service was launched at Harvard University. It is now known as Facebook. At first the site was limited to students there, but ten years later it is now frequented by 1,230 billion monthly active users and has become the world's largest social networking service. *The Social Network*, directed by David
5 Fincher, is the story of Facebook's establishment.
  The story begins with the break-up between Mark Zuckerberg and his girlfriend. In an attempt to divert his mind, he gets drunk and creates Facemash, a website where pictures of female university students were ranked according to their looks. The controversial site became the talk of the campus and soon attracted the attention of the
10 Winklevoss brothers, who had been attempting to make a social networking service for the university. The Winklevoss brothers asked Zuckerberg to help them create a website called Harvard Connection, where Harvard students could share news. Zuckerberg started working on Harvard Connection, and at the same time he worked with his friend Eduardo Saverin to make their own social networking site for students.
15 This site became known as Facebook.
  This is a movie about modern ambitions. The Winklevoss brothers filed a lawsuit accusing Zuckerberg of stealing their website idea. They claimed that Zuckerberg created his own social networking site while stalling on their website. Their lawsuit claimed that their intellectual property was stolen. Intellectual property laws were
20 previously applied to cases where, for example, a writer copied some work from another writer. The Winklevoss lawsuit was one of the first to claim ideas as property.
  The Social Network portrays Mark Zuckerberg as a ruthless entrepreneur. It is unclear whether he actually stole the idea of Facebook from the Winklevoss brothers, but he made some other decisions that damaged his friendships. As Facebook grew bigger,
25 Zuckerberg made plans to share the site with other schools, not just Harvard. In order to do this, he entered into a partnership with Sean Parker, the co-founder of Napster. The contract they agreed between them diluted Saverin's share of Facebook from 33 percent to less than ten percent. Saverin also filed a lawsuit against Zuckerberg for cheating him out of his share of the company. Money is the driving force behind most technology
30 companies, and intellectual property is perhaps the most valuable asset. When large companies approach talented people with talks of acquisition, it is not so much the application itself that they want to buy, it is the talent they are trying to obtain. Zuckerberg, however, resisted the temptation to just become rich. For a long time, he refused to allow advertisements on Facebook and he insisted on offering applications free
35 of charge, even though they were worth a lot of money. Eventually, of course,

Zuckerberg sold shares in Facebook and he became a billionaire, but it could be argued that its autonomy was what made it so valuable.

Comprehension Check

2．本文と内容の一致するものには〇，一致しないものには×をつけなさい。
（1）【　】ザッカーバーグは別れた彼女への嫌がらせとして Facebook を立ち上げた。
（2）【　】サベリンはアイデアを盗用したとしてザッカーバーグを訴えた。
（3）【　】ウィンクルボス兄弟が起こした訴訟は，アイデアを知的財産とみなすものであった。
（4）【　】ザッカーバーグとサベリンは，ショーン・パーカーの株を希薄化させた。
（5）【　】大手企業が才能ある人物に買収話を持ちかけるのは，人材を確保するためである。

For TOEIC

3．Choose the best answer to complete the sentence.

1．Intellectual property laws are applied to cases (　　) a writer copied some work from another writer.
　（A）which　（B）that　（C）where　（D）how

2．Eventually Mark sold shares (　　) Facebook and he became a billionaire.
　（A）on　（B）with　（C）of　（D）in

3．The Winklevoss brothers filed a lawsuit (　　) Zuckerberg of stealing their website idea.
　（A）accuse　（B）accused　（C）accusing　（D）accuses

4．The Winklevoss brothers claimed that Zuckerberg created his own social networking site while (　　) on their website.
　（A）stall　（B）stalled　（C）stalling　（D）was stalling

4. Choose the best answer to each question.

1. Why did Zuckerberg create Facemash?
    (A) To get famous.
    (B) To forget his ex-girlfriend.
    (C) To get a new girlfriend.
    (D) To change his mind.

2. What did the Winklevoss brothers ask Zuckerberg to do?
    (A) Help them launch Facebook
    (B) Help them share news with people all over the world
    (C) Help them dilute Saverine's share of Facebook
    (D) Help them create their website

3. What is this movie about?
    (A) Intellectual property
    (B) Lawsuits
    (C) Money
    (D) Modern ambitions

4. What is NOT indicated about Mark Zuckerberg?
    (A) He is portrayed as a compassionate entrepreneur in this movie.
    (B) He betrayed his friend.
    (C) He was sued by some students at Harvard University.
    (D) He at first didn't place advertisements on his website.

5．Choose the best answer to each question.

1．The (　　) site became the talk of the campus and soon attracted the attention of the Winklevoss brothers, who had been attempting to make a social networking service for the university.
　　（A）disputable　　（B）durable　　（C）conversational　　（D）occasional

2．The Winklevoss brothers asked Zuckerberg (　　) create a website called Harvard Connection, where Harvard students could share news.
　　（A）help them to　　（B）to help them to
　　（C）that he　　（D）helping them

3．Money is the driving force behind most technology companies, and intellectual property is perhaps the most valuable (　　).
　　（A）creation　　（B）complication　　（C）handicap　　（D）commodity

4．For a long time, he refused to allow advertisements on Facebook and he insisted on offering applications free (　　) charge, even though they were worth a lot of money.
　　（A）of　　（B）from　　（C）for　　（D）on

trivia

　『ソーシャル・ネットワーク』は実話に基づくフィクションです。映画の製作は主にエドゥアルド・サベリンへの取材に基づいており，マーク・ザッカーバーグに対する取材は一切行われていません。ザッカーバーグ役を演じたジェシー・アイゼンバーグは事前に彼の映像を研究していましたが，撮影に入るとストーリーや内面の表現に集中するために，独自のマーク・ザッカーバーグ像を作り上げています。これが功を奏して傑作となっているのですが，実際のザッカーバーグはパーティー好きの友好的な人物ですので，勘違いしないようにしておきたいものです。

goofs

　ハーバード大学の学生がフェイスマッシュを使っているとき，Fallout 3 というビデオゲームをしていました。このシーンは 2003 年の設定なのですが，Fallout 3 が発売されるのは 2008 年になってからです。

Unit 11
Psychological Test Subjects

Vocabulary

1. 本文中に登場する次の(1)〜(5)の語彙と同じような意味になるものを，下の(a)〜(e)から選びなさい。

   (1) psychology　　　　　　　（a）罰
   (2) prisoner　　　　　　　　（b）暴　動
   (3) punishment　　　　　　 （c）心理学
   (4) riot　　　　　　　　　　（d）終了する
   (5) terminate　　　　　　　 （e）囚　人
   (6) rebellious　　　　　　　（f）反抗的な

Reading

  The Experiment (2010) is a psychological thriller film starring Adrien Brody and Forest Whitaker. The film follows the behavior of 26 volunteers as they participate in a psychology experiment based in a prison environment. The men have to live in a fake prison for two weeks. If they participate for the full two weeks, they will each be paid 14,000 dollars. However, they must all complete the experiment together. If any individual quits, the experiment will be terminated and everybody will be paid nothing. At the beginning of the experiment the volunteers are divided randomly into two groups: 20 prisoners and six guards. They are given very simple rules to follow: the prisoners must eat three meals every day; the prisoners must be given 30 minutes of recreation time every day; and prisoners must always stay within certain areas. The guards must ensure the prisoners obey the rules at all times. The subjects are told that there are video cameras watching their behavior, and that if any violence occurs the experiment will be terminated and they will all lose their pay.

  The behavior of the volunteers quickly turns bad. The guards punish the prisoners for very minor transgressions. When the experiment is not terminated, the guards conclude that their behavior is acceptable, so they continue to punish the prisoners. At the same time, the prisoners quickly begin to challenge the strict punishments of the guards. They feel the punishments are too severe and that they are being treated unfairly. Eventually there is a violent riot in the prison, and the experiment is terminated. The volunteers leave the fake prison and go home, and they are, after all, paid for their participation.

  The Experiment is a fictional movie, but it is based on a real experiment from 1971. In the real experiment, psychology researchers at Stanford University created a fake prison environment and placed volunteers in it for two weeks. The experiment was terminated after only six days because the subjects' behavior became dangerous. This experiment became famous because its results are interesting. The volunteers assumed the psychologists were observing how the prisoners reacted to being in prison. In fact, the researchers were also observing how the guards reacted to having power over the prisoners. The guards became brutal, aggressive, and abusive. In response, the prisoners became rebellious and defiant.

  The Stanford experiment taught the researchers a lot about the psychology of imprisonment. Social roles influence human behavior in every situation. We are expected to behave a certain way or to avoid certain behavior in our society. Social rules often govern our relationships with others. Teachers and students behave in certain ways: students are expected to accept school rules and follow the teachers' instructions, while teachers are expected to maintain discipline and support the learning environment. The Stanford prison experiment showed the psychologists that unbalanced power in human relationships can make people behave in unexpected ways.

Comprehension Check

2．本文の内容と一致するものには○，一致しないものには×をつけなさい。
(1)【　】映画では被験者が途中で実験を辞退すると，被験者に支払われる報酬は 100 ドル減額される。
(2)【　】映画では監視カメラが，常に被験者の行動を監視していた。
(3)【　】スタンフォード大学の実験では，心理学者は囚人の行動のみを観察していた。
(4)【　】人間の行動が，社会的役割に影響を与える。
(5)【　】映画では実験開始後すぐに，被験者の行動は変わっていった。

For TOEIC

3．Choose the best answer to complete the sentence.

1．*The Experiment* is a fictional movie (　　) is based on a real experiment from 1971.
　　(A) where　　(B) when　　(C) who　　(D) which

2．The participants were (　　) chosen in the experiment.
　　(A) random　　(B) randomly　　(C) randomize　　(D) randomized

3．If any violence occurs, they (　　).
　　(A) were not paid　　(B) have paid　　(C) will pay
　　(D) will not be paid

4．There were a lot of digital cameras (　　) their punishments.
　　(A) watched　　(B) watch　　(C) watching　　(D) have watched

4. Choose the best answer to each question.

1. What is this movie about?
    (A) Love comedy
    (B) Psychological thriller
    (C) Political issue
    (D) International affairs

2. What is the prisoner rule?
    (A) They must not talk with the guards.
    (B) They must stay outside during the recreation time.
    (C) They must eat meals three times a day.
    (D) They must clean their room every day.

3. Why was the experiment terminated in this movie?
    (A) Because one of the prisoners was killed.
    (B) Because the riot occurred.
    (C) Because the prisoners did not follow the rule.
    (D) Because the guards punished the prisoners for a very small mistake.

4. How much money did each participant get paid in this movie?
    (A) 28,000 dollars
    (B) 20,000 dollars
    (C) 14,000 dollars
    (D) 30,000 dollars

5. When was the real experiment conducted?
    (A) 1971
    (B) 2010
    (C) 1890
    (D) 2000

5．Choose the best answer to each question.

1．They feel the punishments are (　　) and that they are being treated unfairly.
　　（A）well　　（B）harsh　　（C）difficult　　（D）critical

2．Psychology researchers at Stanford University created a (　　) prison environment.
　　（A）genuine　　（B）fabric　　（C）false　　（D）imitation

trivia

　この映画は，1971年にアメリカのスタンフォード大学で行われた監獄実験を基に映画化されたものです。実際の実験では，被験者を受刑者役と看守役に分けてそれぞれの役を演じさせましたが，被験者が危険な状態に陥ったためこの実験は6日間で中止されました。実話では普通の大学生などが被験者として実験に参加していましたが，この映画では，さまざまな問題や悩みを抱えた被験者が登場しています。

goofs

　囚人が暴動を起こす場面で，看守役のバリスが受刑者役のトラヴィスをナイフで刺そうとしたとき，トラヴィスはナイフを左手でつかみ，手は血まみれになりました。しかし次の場面，実験の中止を知らせる赤いランプが点灯して，トラヴィスが手を挙げたときには，手には傷痕一つなく血も流れていません。

Unit 12
Aroma

Vocabulary

1. 本文中に登場する次の (1) ～ (7) の語彙と同じような意味になるものを，下の (a) ～ (g) から選びなさい。

　　（1） goers
　　（2） appetite
　　（3） stimulate
　　（4） perfume
　　（5） sniff
　　（6） scratch
　　（7） enhance

　　（a） 匂い，香り
　　（b） 刺激する
　　（c） ニオイを嗅ぐ
　　（d） 引っ掻く
　　（e） 増進する，高める
　　（f） 食　欲
　　（g） （定期的に）参加する観客

Reading

Spy Kids 4D : All the Time in the World is a comedy adventure film starring Jessica Alba, Rowan Blanchard, and Mason Cook. Released in 2011, it is the fourth film in the *Spy Kids* series. The "4D" in the title refers to a fourth dimension: "Aroma-scope". "Aroma-scope" allows members of the audience to smell odors and aromas from the film by scratching aroma cards and sniffing them.

For years film directors have tried to tap into the aromatic effect of odors to enhance the experience for film goers. The first director to try this was Jack Cardiff in his 1960 movie, *Scent of Mystery*. To enable the audience to experience the odors, a system called "Smell-o-Vision" was developed. This piped 30 odors into the seating area of the theater. At various points in the film a specific scent was released to highlight the action on the screen. For example, during one scene, several wine bottles roll down a street and smash against a wall, at which point the smell of wine was released in the theater.

"Smell-o-Vision" was not a success for several reasons. Firstly, the distribution of scents was uneven, so some areas had overpowering odors while others had none. Secondly, the aromas moved around in the air of the theater, so some viewers didn't experience the scent until several seconds after the action on the screen. In general, film goers said that the movie itself wasn't very good, and the strange odors just made it worse.

Since the 1980s, the advertising industry has been perfecting "scratch & sniff" technology. Magazine advertisements for perfume now have a "scratch & sniff" patch where you can sample the aroma directly from the page by scratching the paper's surface to release the scent. This is the basis of the technology used in *Spy Kids 4D : All the Time in the World*. Film goers are handed an "Aroma-scope" card as they enter the theater, and a prompt on the screen tells them when to scratch the numbered patches. While this method may fix some of the problems experienced by the "Smell-o-Vision" audiences of the 1960s, film goers still think the cards are a distraction and are not an essential part of the movie.

Our sense of smell is directly linked to our emotional control center, called the Limbic System. When we inhale a scent, the nerves in our nose send electrical impulses to our brain, and the brain searches our memory for any connections to the scent. The Limbic System is directly connected to the parts of the brain which control our memory, stress levels, heart rate and breathing. Therefore, aromas can directly affect our physiological well-being. Aromas can trigger old memories from many years ago, they can make us feel calm or afraid, and they can either stimulate or suppress our appetite. With such a strong influence over our emotional responses, it is no wonder movie makers continue to try to harness the power of scent.

Comprehension Check

2．本文の内容と一致するものには○，一致しないものには×をつけなさい．
（1）【　】「アロマ・スコープ」というのは，フィルムを舐めることにより，観客にいろいろなニオイやアロマを嗅がせることができるものである．
（2）【　】映画監督たちは映画の観客の体験を向上するために，ニオイという芳香の効果を取り入れたいと試みてきた．
（3）【　】「スメル・オ・ヴィジョン」は，とても効果的だった．
（4）【　】現在香水の雑誌広告には「スクラッチ＆スニフ」のパッチが付いており，ニオイを放出させるために紙の表面を擦ることでページから直接アロマを試すことができる．
（5）【　】我々の臭覚は「辺縁系」と呼ばれる感情をコントロールするセンターに直結している．

For TOEIC

3．Choose the best answer to complete the sentence.

1．*Spy Kids 4D: All the Time* in the World is a comedy adventure film (　　) Jessica Alba, Rowan Blanchard, and Mason Cook.
　　(A) star　　(B) starring　　(C) starred　　(D) had starred

2．For years film directors have tried to (　　) the aromatic effect of odors to enhance the experience for film goers.
　　(A) development　　(B) introduction　　(C) discover　　(D) utilize

3．"Smell-o-Vision" did not (　　) for several reasons.
　　(A) successful　　(B) successive　　(C) succeed　　(D) success

4．Aromas can (　　) old memories from many years ago, they can make us feel calm or afraid.
　　(A) recall　　(B) remember　　(C) make up　　(D) bring back

4．Choose the best answer to each question.

1．What does the "4D" in the title refer to?
（A）a fourth dimension : "Aroma-scope"
（B）a fourth dimension : "Smell-o-Vision"
（C）a fourth dimension : "scratch & sniff"
（D）a fourth dimension : "Scent of Mystery"

2．Who was the first director to try to tap into the aromatic effect to enhance the experience for film goers?
（A）Jessica Alba
（B）Rowan Blanchard
（C）Mason Cook
（D）Jack Cardiff

3．What kind of technology has the advertising industry been perfecting since the 1980s?
（A）"Aroma-scope"
（B）"Smell-o-Vision"
（C）"scratch & sniff"
（D）"Scent of Mystery"

4．What is Our sense of smell directly linked to?
（A）our emotional control center, called the Limbic System
（B）our physical control center, called a prompt on the screen
（C）our body control center, called emotional responses
（D）our brain control center, called the appetite System

5   Choose the best answer to complete the sentence.

1. "Aroma-scope" (   ) members of the audience to smell odors and aromas from the film by scratching aroma cards and sniffing them.
   (A) makes   (B) has   (C) forces   (D) enables

2. This piped 30 odors into the seating area of the theater. At various points in the film a specific scent was (   ) to highlight the action on the screen.
   (A) vanished   (B) developed   (C) sent   (D) changed

3. For example, during one scene, several wine bottles roll down a street and (   ) against a wall, at which point the smell of wine was released in the theater.
   (A) hit   (B) drink   (C) smell   (D) destroy

4. Film goers are handed an "Aroma-scope" card (   ) they enter the theater, and a prompt on the screen tells them when to scratch the numbered patches.
   (A) unless   (B) because   (C) when   (D) once

5. While this method may fix some of the problems experienced by the "Smell-o-Vision" audiences of the 1960s, film goers still think the cards are (   ) and are not an essential part of the movie.
   (A) something that stops you paying attention to what you are doing
   (B) something that makes you paying attention to what you are doing
   (C) something that has you paying attention to what you are doing
   (D) something that pays attention to what you are doing

trivia

　この映画のシリーズ4作品全部に出演しているのは，カルメン・コルテス役のアレクサ・ヴェガとジュニ・コルテス役のダリル・サバラ，そしてイサドール・マチェーテ・コルテス役のダニー・トレホだけです。

goofs

　ティック・トックが子どもたちを一瞬にして動けなくしたとき，犬が二人の間にいたのに，セシルがズームアップされたら犬がいなくなっています。

Unit 13
Dangerous Food Supply

Vocabulary

1. 本文中に登場する次の (1) ～ (7) の語彙と同じような意味になるものを，下の (a) ～ (g) から選びなさい。

  (1) unpalatable　　　　　（a）病　気
  (2) expose　　　　　　　（b）抗生物質
  (3) budget　　　　　　　（c）解体処理する
  (4) disease　　　　　　　（d）不快な
  (5) antibiotics　　　　　　（e）暴露する
  (6) slaughter　　　　　　（f）予　算
  (7) organic　　　　　　　（g）有機栽培の

Reading

Food, Inc. is a documentary film exposing the unpalatable side of food production in the United States of America. Huge multinational corporations are forcing small farms out of business all over the country, and profitability now outweighs both health and environmental concerns. The documentary, directed by Robert Kenner and released in 2008, exposes the dirty secrets of the food industry in the hope that public awareness will generate public demand for better methods.

The documentary looks at the consequences of making profits the priority of the food industry. A low income family is filmed as they shop at a local supermarket. Unfortunately, they find that healthy choices such as fresh vegetables are too expensive for their family budget. The cheapest food is processed or frozen, and therefore full of salt and other preservatives. For many families like this one, the cost of healthy food means that they really have no choice at all when shopping on a budget.

These greedy multinational corporations increase their profits in several ways. One way is to produce processed food abroad, where it can be done more cheaply. Another way is to farm very intensively within the United States. Large factory farms with their Concentrated Animal Feeding Operations (CAFOs) are on the increase. These facilities are noisy, dirty, smelly, and dangerous. The animals live very close together and can spread diseases very easily. Without space and fresh air to keep them healthy, the farmers rely on heavy doses of antibiotics, which remain present in the meat after the animal is slaughtered. Diseases such as E. coli originate in these overcrowded and filthy animal feed lots. The slurry from these feed lots is used to fertilize fields for growing vegetables. In 2006, spinach contaminated with E. coli resulted in 205 illnesses and 3 deaths. More and more consumers are now asking what sort of conditions really exist in our food-producing facilities.

As more consumers express their concern over the filthy conditions of factory farms, hidden cameras are starting to expose the truth about the way our food is produced. In one facility, conditions were so bad that the meat had to be washed with chlorine before it was "fit" for human consumption. As such stories are shared with the general public, many consumers are losing their appetite for food produced on such a large and dangerous scale.

Food, Inc. is only one of a growing number of documentaries and books looking more closely at the business of producing food. One organic farmer, Joel Salatin, suggests that if these massive industrial farms had glass walls open for all to see the ugly truth, the public would quickly demand a completely different food processing system. The documentary concludes with the hopeful message that consumers are not as powerless as they might feel. Since the large corporations' priority is making money, their customers can create change by the informed choices they make at every mealtime. If consumers refuse to pay for the substandard food offered by these corporations, the corporations will be forced to change their methods and produce food that is more palatable to the purchasing public.

Comprehension Check

2．本文の内容と一致するものには○，一致しないものには×をつけなさい。
　　（1）【　】 *Food, Inc.* という映画はアメリカ合衆国の食の安全性をテーマにしたものである。
　　（2）【　】 安価な食料は加工あるいは冷凍されて，大量の砂糖と保存料が投入される。
　　（3）【　】 CAFO を行う工場はとても静かで清潔で安全である。
　　（4）【　】 消費者が安価な食料を生産している工場の実態を知っても，何も変わらないだろう。

For TOEIC

3．Choose the best answer to complete the sentence.

1．*Food, Inc.* is a film that (　　) the unpalatable side of food production in the US.
　　(A) thinks　　(B) consists　　(C) reveals　　(D) makes

2．A low income family is filmed (　　) they are shopping at a local supermarket.
　　(A) after　　(B) before　　(C) because　　(D) while

3．One way multinational corporations increase their profits is (　　) produce processed food abroad, where it can be done more cheaply.
　　(A) as　　(B) for　　(C) in　　(D) to

4．The animals live very close together and can spread diseases (　　).
　　(A) with eases　　(B) of very easy
　　(C) with great ease　　(D) of easiness

Dangerous Food Supply

5. (　　) such stories are shared with the general public, many consumers are losing their appetite for food.
　　(A) Though　(B) Although　(C) Because　(D) In spite of

4. Choose the best answer to each question.

1. Who directed the documentary film released in 2008?
　　(A) Robert De Niro, Jr.
　　(B) Robert Lee Frost
　　(C) Robert Kenner
　　(D) Robert Redford

2. What does a low income family choose when they find that healthy choices are too expensive for their budget?
　　(A) healthy food
　　(B) fresh vegetables
　　(C) expensive food
　　(D) cheap food

3. What does CAFO stand for?
　　(A) Concentrated America Food Opinions
　　(B) Concentrated Animal Food Openers
　　(C) Concentrated America Feed Operations
　　(D) Concentrated Animal Feeding Operation

4. What is Joel Salatin's occupation?
　　(A) He is an organic fixer.
　　(B) He is an organizer.
　　(C) He is an organ farmer.
　　(D) He is an organic farmer.

5. Choose the best answer to complete the sentence.

　　As more consumers express their concern over the filthy conditions of factory farms, hidden (　1　) are starting to expose the truth about the way our food is produced. In one facility, conditions were so bad that the meat had to be washed with chlorine before it was "fit" for human consumption. As such stories are shared with the general public, many consumers are losing their (　2　) for food produced on such a large and dangerous scale. *Food, Inc.* is only one of a growing number of documentaries and books looking more (　3　) at the business of producing food.

1. (A) microphones　　(B) spies　　(C) radios　　(D) video cameras
2. (A) desire　　(B) cooking　　(C) faith　　(D) jobs
3. (A) near　　(B) watching　　(C) closely　　(D) vividly

trivia

　本作品は現代における牛や鶏などの食肉加工産業にスポットをあてているにもかかわらず，本作品の監督でプロデューサーのロバート・ケナー，またジャーナリストで作家でもあるマイケル・ポーランやエリック・シュローサーはいずれも菜食主義者ではないところが面白い。

goofs

　本作品はドキュメンタリーですので，シーンそれ自体に誤りや間違いがあるわけではありません。しかし，本編を通して現代のアメリカに潜む食糧生産事業の実情と実態から，実際は食の安全や健康よりも安価な食品を大量に生産し，販売する企業側の利益追求がクローズアップされています。この大量生産と価格破壊によって，今度は食中毒等を引き起こすこともあります。このことが私たちにとって脅威となり，結局のところ「食」に関する「誤り」を生み出したと言えます。このように今日の誤った「食」を再考するのに有益なドキュメント作品と言えます。

Unit 14
Wolf & Witch-hunting

Vocabulary

1．本文中に登場する次の (1) 〜 (5) の語彙と同じような意味になるものを，下の (a) 〜 (e) から選びなさい。

　　（1）werewolf　　　　　　　　　（a）文　学
　　（2）agreement　　　　　　　　　（b）切断する
　　（3）sever　　　　　　　　　　　（c）人　狼
　　（4）supernatural　　　　　　　　（d）超自然の
　　（5）literature　　　　　　　　　（e）合　意

Reading

Red Riding Hood is a horror romance starring Amanda Seyfried and produced by Leonardo Di Caprio. The movie is loosely based on the European folk tale *Little Red Riding Hood*, which was collected by the Brothers Grimm and included in their *Grimms' Fairy Tales*. This story differs from the old folk tale by including the legend of the werewolf. In the original story, Red Riding Hood is hunted by a real wolf. In this story, she is hunted by a werewolf.

Valerie is a young woman caught in a love triangle. Valerie is in love with Peter, but her parents have arranged for her to marry Henry. Valerie's sister, Lucie, is in love with Henry, but her parents will not give her permission to marry him. The villagers live in fear of a werewolf, but they have an agreement that he will not hunt people as long as they give him cows and sheep to eat. When Lucie is killed by the werewolf everyone in the village knows that the agreement is over, and they decide to hunt the werewolf.

The villagers ask a famous monster hunter (Father Solomon) to help them kill the werewolf and he arrives with bad news. Usually, the werewolf simply kills its prey, but occasionally it makes new werewolves. Once every thirteen years, during the "Blood Moon", the werewolf's bite does not kill, instead, it infects the victim and transforms him or her into a werewolf, and now is the time of the Blood Moon. Silver kills werewolves, and Father Solomon has coated his fingernails with silver so he can fight them. During a fight, the werewolf bites off his hand. Father Solomon is now infected, because of the Blood Moon, and must be killed. But Valerie takes his severed hand to use as a weapon.

Valerie goes to hunt the werewolf and meets Peter in the forest. She learns that the werewolf is really her father, and he wants her to leave the village with him. It is the Blood Moon time and he wants to bite her, turn her into a werewolf, and then they can go and live somewhere far away. Valerie refuses and tries to escape. Peter tries to help her and he is bitten. They both know that he will now become a werewolf, but Valerie is not afraid of him. Together, they kill Valerie's father, she stabs him with Father Solomon's severed hand, using his silver fingernails like daggers. In the end, Valerie marries Peter and keeps his secret, but they have to live in the forest because she can't go back to the village.

Red Riding Hood has all the elements of Gothic horror and Classical romance. The image of an isolated village besieged by a supernatural monster appears in many European folk tales. Similarly, the romantic drama of being forbidden to marry for love, and discovering secrets about parents is seen frequently in classic European literature.

Comprehension Check

2．本文の内容と一致するものには〇，一致しないものには×をつけなさい。
　　（1）【　　】この物語は，グリム童話だけに基づいている。
　　（2）【　　】ヴァレリーとピーターは，親から結婚を認められた。
　　（3）【　　】赤い月の頃，人狼が噛むと，獲物は人狼になった。
　　（4）【　　】ヴァレリーは，切断された神父の銀の手で，人狼を殺した。
　　（5）【　　】ヴァレリーとピーターは，結婚して村で幸せに暮らした。

For TOEIC

3．Choose the best answer to complete the sentence.

1．The movie is loosely （　　）（　　） the European folk tale.
　　（A）base on　　（B）based on　　（C）basis on　　（D）based in

2．He was （　　）（　　）（　　） her at the first sight.
　　（A）fall in love　　（B）take care of　　（C）lots of love
　　（D）in love with

3．He （　　）（　　）（　　） and lost face.
　　（A）made his promise　　（B）kept his promise
　　（C）broke his promise　　（D）gave his word

4．（　　）（　　）（　　） the princess became happy.
　　（A）In the end　　　（B）The whole time
　　（C）At this moment　（D）To this end

5．He will finish his homework quickly （　　） he can spend more time playing computer games.
　　（A）but　　（B）so　　（C）only　　（D）if

4. Choose the best answer to each question.

1. What is this movie about?
   (A) Horror romance
   (B) Adventure story
   (C) Comic story
   (D) Love Comedy

2. What is *Little Red Riding Hood* is included in?
   (A) Blood Moon
   (B) Grimms' Fairy Tales
   (C) Classical Romance
   (D) Aesop's Fables

3. Why does everyone in village know the agreement with the werewolf is over?
   (A) Because it is the "Blood Moon."
   (B) Because Father Solomon arrives with bad news.
   (C) Because everyone in the village lives in fear of a werewolf.
   (D) Because Lucy is killed by the werewolf.

4. Who is the werewolf?
   (A) Henry
   (B) Valerie
   (C) Valerie's father
   (D) Father Solomon

5. What is frequently seen in classic European literature?
   (A) The girl hunted by a real wolf
   (B) Discovering secrets about parents
   (C) Fingernails coated with silver
   (D) A woman monster hunter

5. Choose the best answer to each question.

　　Valerie is a young woman who finds herself in a love triangle. (1) Valerie and Peter love each other, her parents won't permit her to marry him and arrange for her to marry Henry instead. (2) the villagers are afraid of the werewolf, they agree with him that he won't kill any villagers, (3) they bring him cows and sheep to eat. When Lucie is killed by the werewolf, villagers know that (4) efforts they make, in the end it is useless.

1．(A) As　　(B) Even though　　(C) Because　　(D) Now that
2．(A) Although　　(B) Until　　(C) As　　(D) If
3．(A) as well as　　(B) as soon as　　(C) as if　　(D) as long as
4．(A) whether　　(B) even if
　　(C) no matter how　　(D) no matter what

trivia

　バレリーの恋人ピーターの名前は，1936年ロシアのセルゲイ・プロコフィエフが子ども向けに作った音楽童話，「ピーターと狼」から取られたもの。この作品も狼が出てくるので，ぴったりの名前ですね。

goofs

　ピーターの髪型は，中世ヨーロッパでは見られない，現代風の髪型です。ジェルを使っていない時代に，下に落ちてこないよう重力に必死に逆らっている髪型です。

Unit 15
Self-searching Journey

Vocabulary

1. 本文中に登場する次の(1)〜(7)の語彙と同じような意味になるものを下の(a)〜(g)から選びなさい。

    (1) account   (a) 評論家
    (2) career   (b) 洞 察
    (3) ashram   (c) 祈 り
    (4) meditation   (d) 瞑 想
    (5) prayer(s)   (e) (ヒンズー教の) 修行所
    (6) insight(s)   (f) 経 歴
    (7) critic(s)   (g) 話, 説明, 記述

Reading

Eat, Pray, Love is a romantic comedy drama starring Julia Roberts and produced by Dede Gardner. It was released in 2010, following the worldwide success of Elizabeth Gilbert's bestselling book of the same name. This is an autobiographical account of Gilbert's travels around the world after she got divorced.

Elizabeth Gilbert is 32 years old, well educated, and has a successful career as a writer and journalist. Despite her outward success, inwardly she feels very different. She questions her abilities and the things she has faith in, and gradually becomes more and more lost and confused. She never talks to her husband about how she feels until, eventually, she tells him she wants to end their marriage.

Following her divorce, Gilbert tries dating again, but finds it difficult, and breaking up leaves her feeling shocked and alone. She realizes that the problem lies inside herself, not outside in the world. She decides she needs to get away from her life, to go away somewhere and discover what is really important to her. She leaves behind all the things she has accumulated and embarks on a journey of self-discovery.

Gilbert spends a whole year traveling around the world. By necessity, she leaves behind most of her possessions ; she has to carry everything she needs in her bag, so she has to think carefully about which things she really needs. She goes to Italy where she learns to speak Italian and explores Italian food. During her four months in Italy she discovers the true pleasure of eating good food that doesn't come in packets. Next, she spends three months in India, where she enters an ashram and learns meditation. The ashram is not comfortable, the food is very basic, and there are mosquitoes everywhere. Nevertheless, she learns to be peaceful and to concentrate on her meditations and prayers. She spends the remainder of her year on the Indonesian island of Bali. While studying with a medicine man and searching for more insights into her true self, she unexpectedly falls in love. She meets a Brazilian businessman named Felipe and, enjoying her new-found inner peace, realizes that she can now balance a loving relationship with taking care of herself.

Eat, Pray, Love has received mixed reviews from critics. Some say the story is too simple and that it sounds like romantic fiction. Others say the actual story is quite boring and Gilbert had to add funny stories to make it more interesting. Regardless of the reviews, however, this has become one of the most famous movies in recent years, and many people have enjoyed its message of finding peace and joy in everyday life.

Comprehension Check

2．本文の内容と一致するものには○，一致しないものには×をつけなさい。
（1）【　】この映画はエリザベス・ギルバートの自伝に基づいている。
（2）【　】エリザベス・ギルバートはジャーナリストとしては成功していない。
（3）【　】問題は自分にあるのではなく，自分の周りにあるとギルバートは思っている。
（4）【　】ギルバートはイタリアで心の平穏をつかむ。
（5）【　】この映画は日常生活の中に平穏と喜びを見つけることの大切さを伝えている。

For TOEIC

3．Choose the best answer to complete the sentence.

1．The publication of this book (　　) by the release of the movie with the same title.
　　（A）followed　　（B）following　　（C）follows　　（D）was followed

2．While (　　) in London, he visited as many museums as possible.
　　（A）his stay　　（B）staying　　（C）stay　　（D）stayed

3．(　　) in France, she can make herself understood in French.
　　（A）Educate　　（B）Educated　　（C）Educating　　（D）Education

4．The movie is rather (　　), although the original story is a lot of fun.
　　（A）disappoint　　（B）disappointed
　　（C）disappointing　　（D）disappointment

5．She spent three months (　　) for the wedding ceremony and reception.
　　（A）to prepare　　（B）prepared　　（C）preparing　　（D）preparation

Self-searching Journey　　87

4. Choose the best answer to each question.

1. What is this movie about?
    (A) Environmental issues
    (B) Science fiction
    (C) A tragic story
    (D) A love comedy

2. What was Elizabeth Gilbert's job before her divorce?
    (A) A newspaper reporter
    (B) A writer-journalist
    (C) A world traveler
    (D) A businesswoman

3. What does Gilbert learn in Italy?
    (A) Inner peace
    (B) Meditation
    (C) True self
    (D) Speaking Italian

4. How long does Gilbert stay on the island of Bali?
    (A) Three months
    (B) Four months
    (C) Five months
    (D) Six months

5. What does Gilbert find after she meets a Brazilian businessman?
    (A) Inner peace
    (B) A loving relationship
    (C) Meditations
    (D) True pleasure

5．Choose the best answer to each question.

1．(　　) her outward success, inwardly she feels very different.
　　(A) In spite of
　　(B) In addition to
　　(C) In terms of
　　(D) With respect to

2．She (　　) on a journey of self-discovery.
　　(A) gets in　　(B) gets off　　(C) sets in　　(D) sets out

3．She spends the (　　) of her year on the Indonesian island of Bali.
　　(A) rest　　(B) half　　(C) others　　(D) most

trivia

　映画のなかで出てくるピザ屋さんは，イタリアのナポリにある実在のお店です。ピザを食べているジュリア・ロバーツの後ろに見える白い服の男性はこのお店の創始者 Michele Condurro, の孫にあたるひとで，Antonio Condurro といいます。

goofs

　リズが倉庫の前に立っていたとき，彼女の弁護士から電話がかかってきますが，着信音がし始める前にポケットの携帯を手で取ろうとしています。

Unit 16
Travelling in Space

Vocabulary

1. 本文中に登場する次の(1)〜(7)の語彙と同じような意味になるものを，下の(a)〜(g)から選びなさい。

　　（1）gravity　　　　　　　　　　（a）神　話
　　（2）astronaut　　　　　　　　　（b）映画撮影術
　　（3）myth　　　　　　　　　　　（c）生命維持に必要な
　　（4）cinematography　　　　　　（d）宇宙飛行士
　　（5）vital　　　　　　　　　　　（e）残　骸
　　（6）debris　　　　　　　　　　（f）機能しなくなった
　　（7）defunct　　　　　　　　　　（g）重　力

Reading

Gravity is a science fiction drama starring Sandra Bullock and George Clooney. The movie was released in 2013, and in 2014 it won seven Academy Awards, also called "Oscars". The plot is quite simple : two astronauts are stranded in space when there is an accident on their shuttle. However, the drama is very moving as the two astronauts try to survive a situation that appears to be hopeless.

People have always been fascinated by the stars. Since ancient times, all cultures have told stories about the stars, and created myths about space. People have always wondered about the nature of our world, and have looked to space to find answers. The desire to see and understand the stars more clearly has motivated many generations of scientists to develop space technology. Astronomers have developed powerful telescopes to observe the stars from Earth, and engineers have developed spacecraft to transport humans into space. Now we have satellites and space stations, allowing people to stay in space for longer and gather more information.

In 1969, the first humans walked on the moon. The images were transmitted from space and watched on television all over the world. Everyone was fascinated by the images of astronauts bouncing in slow motion on the moon's surface, where there is very little gravity. Since then, we have become very familiar with images of people moving around in zero gravity environments, both in documentaries and in fictional films. Despite our familiarity with such images, *Gravity* won Oscars for both cinematography and visual effects. The portrayal of people moving in zero gravity was outstanding, even though we are no longer surprised by it. The movie was made using a combination of live-action filming and computer generated imagery (CGI). The production company was forced to invent new camera techniques to create images that nobody had ever seen before. For this reason, the movie also won an Oscar for film editing.

There are many dangers related to traveling in space. Of course, there is no air to breathe or water to drink, so maintaining the spacecraft is vital. However, there are other dangers, too. In *Gravity*, debris from a defunct satellite crashes into the space shuttle while the two astronauts are conducting a spacewalk in their spacesuits. Their shuttle is destroyed and they are left floating in space with only the air remaining in their oxygen tanks. Although the movie is a work of science fiction, the dangers posed by space debris are very real.

Gravity captured the imagination of movie audiences all over the world. The idea of being stranded in space is terrifying, the challenge of finding a solution is thrilling, and the performance of the leading actors is outstanding. As our fascination with the stars continues, it is possible that movies like *Gravity* will influence people to care more about the space environment, and keep it safe for future generations of space explorers.

Comprehension Check

2．本文の内容と一致するものには〇，一致しないものには×をつけなさい。
　（1）【　】*Gravity* はサンドラ・ブロックとジョージ・クルーニー主演のSFドラマで，2013年にアカデミー賞7部門を受賞した。
　（2）【　】天文学者は地上から星を観測するために強力な望遠鏡を発達させ，エンジニアは人類を宇宙へ運ぶために宇宙船を発達させてきた。
　（3）【　】1959年に，初めて人類が月面を歩いた。
　（4）【　】*Gravity* は映画撮影法と視覚効果の両方でオスカーを受賞した。

For TOEIC

3．Choose the best answer to complete the sentence.

1．*Gravity* is a science fiction drama (　　) Sandra Bullock and George Clooney.
　（A）star　（B）starring　（C）starred　（D）has starred

2．The movie was (　　) in 2013.
　（A）make　（B）making　（C）made　（D）being made

3．People have always (　　) about the nature of our world.
　（A）think　（B）thinks　（C）thought　（D）being thought

4．Everyone was fascinated (　　) the images of astronauts bouncing in slow motion on the moon's surface.
　（A）off　（B）though　（C）away　（D）by

5．There are many dangers related (　　) traveling in space.
　（A）from　（B）to　（C）how　（D）what

4. Choose the best answer to each question.

1. Who are stranded in space when there is an accident on their shuttle ?
    (A) two astronomers
    (B) three aquanauts
    (C) three pilots
    (D) two astronauts

2. When did the first humans walk on the moon ?
    (A) in 2013
    (B) in 2014
    (C) in 1959
    (D) in 1969

3. Why is maintaining the spacecraft vital ?
    (A) Because there is air to breathe and water to drink.
    (B) Because there is no gas to breathe or oil to drink.
    (C) Because there are no spaceships or rockets.
    (D) Because there is no air to breathe or water to drink.

4. What kind of costume is needed for conducting a spacewalk ?
    (A) bathing suit
    (B) fatigue jacket
    (C) gym suit
    (D) spacesuit

5. Choose the best answer to complete the sentence.

1. People have always been fascinated by the stars. (　　) ancient times, all cultures have told stories about the stars, and created myths about space.
　　(A) After　　(B) Before　　(C) On　　(D) From

2. Everyone was fascinated by the images of astronauts bouncing in slow motion on the moon's surface, (　　) there is very little gravity.
　　(A) which　　(B) what　　(C) that　　(D) where

3. As our fascination with the stars continues, it is possible that movies like Gravity will influence people to (　　) more about the space environment, and keep it safe for future generations of space explorers.
　　(A) cure　　(B) worry　　(C) be observed　　(D) be concerned

trivia

　宇宙管制センターの画面外の声はエド・ハリスのもので，彼は『アポロ13号』（1995年）のときの管制官ジーン・クランツと，映画『ライトスタッフ』（1983年）のジョン・グレンの役を演じた俳優です。

goofs

　コワルスキーが「ソユーズ」のことを言及するときに，最初は正しく"Soyuz"と発音していたのに，次のときには"*SoyEZ.*"と間違った発音をしています。

作品の紹介
原題／邦題
（制作年）

Country Strong／カントリー・ストロング（2010）
 監督：シャナ・フェステ
 制作会社：ソニー・ピクチャーズエンタテインメント
 DVD 販売元：ソニー・ピクチャーズエンタテインメント

Tangled／塔の上のラプンツェル（2010）
 監督：バイロン・ハワード／ネイサン・グレノ
 制作会社：ウォルト・ディズニー・アニメーション・スタジオ
 DVD 販売元：ウォルト・ディズニー・ジャパン株式会社

Life of Pi／ライフ・オブ・パイ／トラと漂流した 227 日（2012）
 監督：アン・リー
 制作会社：フォックス 2000 ピクチャーズ
 DVD 販売元：20 世紀フォックス・ホーム・エンターテイメント・ジャパン

Hugo／ヒューゴの不思議な発明（2011）
 監督：マーティン・スコセッシ
 制作会社：GK フィルムズ／インフィニタム・ニヒル
 DVD 販売元：パラマウント・ホーム・エンタテインメント・ジャパン

No Impact Man／地球にやさしい生活（2009）
 監督：ローラ・ガバート／ジャスティン・シャイン
 制作国：アメリカ
 DVD 販売元：紀伊國屋書店

The Karate Kid／ベスト・キッド（2010）
 監督：ハラルド・ズワルト
 制作会社：オーバーブック・エンターテインメント／JW プロダクションズ／中国電影集団公司
 DVD 販売元：ソニー・ピクチャーズエンタテインメント

The Amazing Spider-Man／アメイジング・スパイダーマン（2012）
 監督：マーク・ウェブ
 制作会社：マーベル・エンターテインメント／ローラ・ジスキンプロダクション
 DVD 販売元：ソニー・ピクチャーズエンタテインメント

The King's Speech／英国王のスピーチ（2010）

監督：トム・フーパー
　　制作会社：シー・ソウ・フィルムズ／ベッドラム・プロダクションズ
　　DVD 販売元：Happinet（SB）（D）

Moneyball／マネーボール（2011）
　　監督：ベネット・ミラー
　　制作会社：マイケル・デ・ルカ・プロダクションズ／スコット・ルーディン・プロダクションズ／スペシャルティ・フィルムズ
　　DVD 販売元：ソニー・ピクチャーズエンタテインメント

The Social Network／ソーシャル・ネットワーク（2010）
　　監督：デヴィッド・フィンチャー
　　制作会社：レラティビティ・メディア／トリガー・ストリート・プロダクション
　　DVD 販売元：ソニー・ピクチャーズエンタテインメント

The Experiment／エクスペリメント（2010）
　　監督：ポール・T・シュアリング
　　制作国：アメリカ
　　DVD 販売元：Happinet（SB）（D）

Spy Kids 4D : All the Time in the World／スパイキッズ 4D：ワールドタイム・ミッション（2011）
　　監督：ロバート・ロドリゲス
　　制作会社：トラブル・メーカー・スタジオズ
　　DVD 販売元：SHOCHIKU Co., Ltd.（SH）（D）

Food, Inc.／フード・インク（2008）
　　監督：ロバート・ケナー
　　制作国：アメリカ
　　DVD 販売元：紀伊國屋書店

Red Riding Hood／赤ずきん（2011）
　　監督：キャサリン・ハードウィック
　　制作会社：アピアン・ウェイ・プロダクション
　　DVD 販売元：ワーナー・ホーム・ビデオ

Eat, Pray, Love／食べて，祈って，恋をして（2010）
　　監督：ライアン・マーフィー
　　制作会社：プラン B エンターテインメント
　　DVD 販売元：ソニー・ピクチャーズエンタテインメント

Gravity／ゼロ・グラビティ（2013）
　　監督：アルフォンソ・キュアロン
　　制作会社：ヘイデイ・フィルムズ
　　DVD 販売元：ワーナー・ホーム・ビデオ

映画で学ぶ 英語を楽しむ
English Delight of Movie English and TOEIC

2015年4月20日　初版第1刷発行	〈検印省略〉
	定価はカバーに表示しています

<table>
<tr><td>編　　者</td><td>高　瀬　文　広</td></tr>
<tr><td>英文校閲</td><td>Kate Parkinson</td></tr>
<tr><td>発行者</td><td>杉　田　啓　三</td></tr>
<tr><td>印刷者</td><td>林　　初　彦</td></tr>
</table>

発行所　株式会社　ミネルヴァ書房
607-8494 京都市山科区日ノ岡堤谷町1
電話 (075)581-5191／振替 01020-0-8076

Ⓒ高瀬ほか，2015　　太洋社・藤沢製本

ISBN978-4-623-07349-8
Printed in Japan

よくわかる翻訳通訳学

鳥飼玖美子編著　　　　　　　　　　　　　　　B 5 判 200 頁　本体 2400 円

翻訳通訳の魅力的な世界を存分に味わえる入門書。大学の講義用テキストとして翻訳通訳学の全体像が把握できるよう工夫。また，翻訳や通訳について知りたい，通訳者や翻訳者に興味のある人に最適な書。

よくわかる異文化コミュニケーション

池田理知子編著　　　　　　　　　　　　　　　B 5 判 202 頁　本体 2500 円

異質な他者との出会いは，驚きや発見をもたらし，それが当たり前のものとして見過ごしていたことの見直しにつながる。そうした他者とどのような〈関係性＝コミュニケーション〉を構築していくかが，「異文化コミュニケーション」の主題である。本書は，既存の理論や研究成果の検証をとおして，新たな視点を提示した入門書。

アメリカ文化 55 のキーワード

笹田直人・野田研一・山里勝己編著　　　　　　A 5 判　298 頁　本体 2500 円

アメリカ文化とは何か。本書は，文学作品，美術，映画，音楽など多様なメディアを介しつつ，アメリカのさまざまな〈文化〉的特徴を，「具体的なモノ・コト」という特定の視点から読み解く。

イギリス文化 55 のキーワード

木下　卓・窪田憲子・久森和子編著　　　　　　A 5 判　296 頁　本体 2400 円

シェイクスピアからビートルズ，ロンドン塔からパブ，紳士からスパイまで，文化の織りなす物語。古くて新しい，新しくて古いイギリス文化を知る必携の一冊。

フランス文化 55 のキーワード

朝比奈美知子・横山安由美編著　　　　　　　　A 5 判　292 頁　本体 2500 円

「歴史」「フランス的精神」「芸術」「生活」「現代社会」「パリ」「さまざまな地方」という七つの章により構成。フランスの彩り豊かな魅力をコンパクトに紹介し，図版も多数掲載。本書のキーワードを読み進めると，フランスのたどった歴史が見えてくる。

―― ミネルヴァ書房 ――
http://www.minervashobo.co.jp